INTO THE LIGHT

In His Love & Truth

Phil 1:29

[signature]

8/25/2008

Into the Light

Steven Masood

Biblical Quotations are from the Authorized Version.
Qur'anic references are taken from Muhammad Marmaduke
Pickthal, *The Meaning of the Glorious Qur'an* (Karachi: Taj
Company, n.d)

Library of Congress Cataloging-in-Publication Data

A catalogue record for this book is available from the
Library of Congress

ISBN 978-1-934447-11-6

Printed in the United States of America

Contents

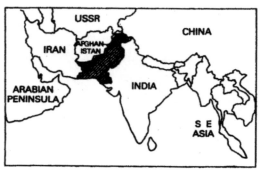

The Dream

I came to the crossroads, a lost and weeping boy. I asked the passers-by which road would lead to my home, but no one could tell me. Finally, I chose a road at random and walked on, desolate.

I was hungry, and as I walked I saw a beautiful garden with laden fruit trees. The garden had a high boundary wall and before me stood a big gate, closed. I tried repeatedly, but I could not open it.

I cried out, "Please open the gate. I'm so hungry. I have to buy some fruit. I have money and I am hungry. Please open to me!" In front of me the gate swung silently open.

In the garden some children were playing. I went up to them. Seeing me, they stopped and I told them, "I have forgotten my way home. If I get home late my parents will beat me." As I watched, a child took a bite from his apple. I looked at him and repeated, "I am very hungry."

The children called out, "Daddy, see who has come!" I turned, and there among the bushes I saw an old, old man, but healthy and strong, coming towards us. I had the strange feeling that he was my Daddy too! And yet, suddenly, I became afraid and turned to run away, but his voice stopped me.

"My son! My child! I am not angry with you. You are my child like these others."

His voice was not my father's voice, but I turned to him, and then I was in his arms, and he was holding me. The other children crowded round and kissed me. They gave me fruit from their baskets and told me about the old man, their Father, and how he loved. I begged them to let me live with them since I felt so unloved in my own home.

"Please let me live with you. I will go to school with you, and I'm sure the teacher will not beat me as Muhammad Ismail does!"

Father smiled at me, "Son, I have asked Muhammad Ismail not to beat you. I have told him that he is to take care of you for you are a good child."

I clung to him and buried my face in his white garments.

"No, Daddy. I will live here with you."

"Son," he said to me gently "You are a good child, and good children obey their Father. Go back to that school now, and when you have finished your studies there, I will see that you are admitted to my school. Come on now. Let me take you to your home."

Ahmadiyya Muslim Childhood

I was born at the time of *fajr*, dawn, the time for the morning-prayer. In our strong religious tradition, this was regarded as very auspicious.

Ashhadun La Ilaha illallah (I bear witness that there is no god but Allah); *Muhammadar – Rasulullah* (Muhammad is the apostle of Allah).

As my father held me and whispered these words in my ear that confirmed my place in the Muslim world of my forebears, he was glad. Here, in the home of her parents, as tradition prescribed, his new wife had given him another son! No doubt my mother felt fulfilled in her new role as the mother of her husband's son, for sons are highly prized in Muslim society. Many are the prayers that are prayed for the gift of sons; few are the prayers for daughters.

They named me Masood Ahmad Khan. Ahmad was the other name of the Prophet Muhammad, and it is from this name that our Ahmadiyya community derived its name. In such a setting it was a privilege to bear the name of Ahmad.

The morning of November 30, 1951, was cool in Tarnab in the northern part of Pakistan, some thirty miles from Peshawar. My mother's parents were

9

wealthy landowners and leased their lands to tenant farmers who tilled the fields. In return for use of his land, the farmers would pay a portion of the crops they raised to my grandfather. Unfortunately, my grandfather was not wise, and eventually he lost control of his lands—but that is another story.

At the time of my birth, Grandfather was the head of a large extended family of about twenty-five members. He had a number of daughters and only one son. The first three or four years of my life were spent in his house, and I remember it, as a child will, as an enormous building. It was constructed of mud bricks, like the other houses in the area, and was cool inside. The house contained some ten or fifteen rooms built around a courtyard. Around the outside was a deep veranda that shaded the rooms from the sun in the hot weather, and beyond the veranda grape vines stretched into the distance. I thought it was a wonderful house, and I was sad to leave it. Later, when I was about seven years old, I went there again with my parents, but that was the last time.

Grandfather had his private mosque on his land as did many wealthy landlords at that time. Even today it is not uncommon. From there, five times a day, the *adhan*, the call to prayer, would sound, and we would all stop and pray.

Allah-o-Akhar, Allaho Akbar ...

God is great, God is great

Ashhado anna Muhammadar-Rasuluilah ...

I bear witness that Muhammad is the Messenger of God ...

Come to prayer ... No one is worthy of worship but Allah.

The voice of the *muezzin*, the one who calls the Muslim faithful to prayer, would echo around the estate, especially in the early morning when it was quiet and cool. The echoes seemed to go on and on. It was a comfortable world for a child. I was secure in the love of my large family, all living there together. In those early years, it was largely a woman's world in which I lived, but that is true for everyone brought up in a Muslim country. Only later did men begin to take a larger place in my life. My father was often away, then, as later. He always seemed to be traveling somewhere. No one seemed to know where he went, and though I loved him, he was not an important part of family life in those early years.

My father was born in Afghanistan. His family had been important in their village in that hidden land; my paternal grandfather had been a religious leader there. He died when my father was just a few months old, and soon after my grandmother also died. For some years, my father continued to live with his mother's brother (my great-uncle) in that village, but when he was about thirteen something happened that was to change his life permanently.

Apparently, my father had inherited quite a lot of property, orchards, and gardens when my grandfather died, and this uncle had been looking after it in trust for my father. However, when he began to grow up, some people came to him one day and told him that his uncle planned to kill him to get the lands for himself! My father was frightened, but it was not until about two years later that he finally ran away.

He came to Quetta, a large city near the southeast border of Afghanistan. Quetta was then in India, but later became part of Pakistan after Partition in 1947.

Here my father met a kind Ahmadi missionary who took pity on him and brought him into his own home. Eventually, he was married to this good man's daughter and several children were born to them.

One night in 1935, a great earthquake leveled the mud-brick city of Quetta, and some sixty-thousand people were killed. Among them were my father's wife and at least two of his children. Amazingly, when the house collapsed my father was shielded from the falling rubble by a door that covered his body; because of this, I am alive today!

When I was born, Father was employed as a bodyguard to the *Khalifa*, or Successor, the leader of the Ahmadi sect of Islam. This was not his only source of income, however. He tried many different things. At one time he ran a small electrical shop, and then he started his own shoe factory. This trade he learned while in Quetta as it was necessary for Ahmadi missionaries to learn such skills. My friends sometimes teased me, calling me a "son of a cobbler."

The Ahmadis, as they call themselves, number perhaps as many as twelve million. Most of them live in Pakistan, though there are some sizeable communities in other parts of the world where Ahmadi missionaries have taken the teaching of their founder, Mirza Ghulam Ahmad, notably West Africa and South-East Asia.

Ghulam Ahmad was born in about 1835 and came from Qadian, a town that is some seventy miles from Lahore, just east of the present-day Pakistani border, in India. He was a most devout Muslim and longed to see Islam revitalized. He began, in the 1880s, to have dreams and visions about this and became convinced that he was the promised Messiah who is prophesied in the books of most world religions, including the Bible, the Holy Book of the Christians. He claimed to have come in the spirit and power of Jesus Christ (the Prophet *Isa*), but despite this, he had very little regard for Christians, the followers of Jesus Christ.

In every major respect except two, Ahmadis hold orthodox Muslim beliefs. Muslims believe that Muhammad was the last and greatest of the prophets of God, whereas Ahmadis claim that Ghulam Ahmad must be given a special place as the Messiah-Leader and that without this, faith is incomplete. Orthodox Muslims believe that Jesus did not die on the cross and that—he ascended into heaven. Ahmadis hold that he died in Kashmir and claim that his tomb may be seen there today. Ghulam Ahmad taught that Jesus was crucified but that he was taken down from the cross before he died, then being revived with a special ointment before going to Kashmir, only to die there at 120 years of age.

Some of these distinctive Ahmadi doctrines were later to prove to be the very things about which the Spirit of Truth enlightened me during my search for the truth.

After the death of Ghulam Ahmad, a dispute arose among his followers. Some felt that he was simply a *mujaddid*, a reformer, who had come to purify Islam, while others were sure that he was a prophet and indeed the Messiah, the Mahdi (leader) who had been promised. By 1914, six years after Ghulam Ahmad's death, an open split had occurred. The second group appointed the son of Ghulam Ahmad, Bashir-u-Din, second *Khalifa* and made their headquarters in Qadian, Ghulam Ahmad's old village. They became known as the Qadiani party by those who opposed them, and were the larger group. The smaller group went off to Lahore, now the second-biggest city in Pakistan, and they are known as the Lahore party.

My father was a Qadiani man, heart and soul. He moved to Qadian sometime after the death of his first wife, and I know that he married at least two more wives there in the 1940s. In 1947 when India was divided into India and Pakistan at the time of Independence, my father along with many other Ahmadis, moved to Lahore to be in Pakistan. As Muslims, they felt that they would not be safe in India, and indeed, thousands of Muslims were killed as they tried to escape into Pakistan. But once again, God kept my father safe. By the time my father married my mother in 1950 he already had a large family. I sometimes feel that this may have been the greatest trouble in my father's life! He seemed always to hope that, by taking another wife, his fortunes would change, and he would become wealthy. He never did.

As a child I knew none of this. By the time we moved to Rabwah, when I was about ten years old, it had become the main centre of the Qadiani Ahmadis. Rabwah was a new town, founded in 1951, and was so strongly Qadiani that until 1974 no non-Ahmadi could live there. It was in Rabwah that I was brought up.

From the beginning my education had been grounded in the Qur'an. We were People of the Book and took pride in learning the Holy Book of the Muslims by heart. By the time I was ten, I had learned long portions of the Qur'an by heart and two years later memorized the whole of it. All Muslim children learn the Qur'an in Arabic, for that is the language in which it is believed that Muhammad received it, but our own language was Urdu.

The Holy Books for a Muslim are the *Torah* (the law), the *Zabur* (the psalms), the *Injil* (the gospel) and the Qur'an. Their stories were familiar to me from the earliest age; Noah and Abraham were like old friends. The set prayers of the day were the accents of our lives, and the discipline of these times taught me faithfulness.

> I believe in God; I believe in His Prophets; I believe in His angels; I believe in His Books; I believe in the Day of Judgment.

> I thank God who is the God of the Universe. He is merciful and great to us. He is a gracious God, and He owns the Day of Judgment. Show us the way of the people You have blessed, O Lord, and do not let us go astray and become as those who have disbelieved. O God, accept this prayer. Amen.

I remember that until I was seven years old, every night before going to sleep such prayers in Arabic I would pray with my mother, when she was available, or even with my father. As a child, I would pray either in my bedroom or theirs.

"Mother, I want to sleep. It's time to pray."

"Right, son, I will hear you pray," my mother would reply.

Sometimes I would go to my parents' bedroom for prayer and find them quarreling. It was usually about some financial or family problem, and on one occasion it was about my father's frequent absences.

One night, after overhearing yet another argument between my parents about one of my father's other wives, I remember thinking, "When I grow up and am big enough, I will have only *one* wife!"

Prayer was the clock of our lives. Every morning before sunrise, at dawn – *fajr,* we would call on Allah.

The *Zuhr*, or noon prayer, punctuated the day with its duties and routines, then one hour before sunset we would be called to prayer again. Just as the sun went down we prayed yet again, and the final prayer of the day was around eight o'clock in the evening, but this was not a strict requirement as were the other prayer times in the day.

One thing had puzzled me from early on when I prayed, and when I was about ten years old I realized what it was. When I prayed before I went to bed, I was taught to pray for God's blessing for Muhammad:

O God, bless Muhammad and the descendants of Muhammad, even as you blessed Abraham and his descendants.

"But," I reasoned, "if Muhammad is such a blessing for the world, then why do we ask God to bless him?" Even though I was so young this confused me, for it did not seem to make sense.

Then there was the formula whereby, when we mentioned Muhammad, we would add the words, "peace be upon him." Again, I wondered, did he have no peace; why must we request this for him? If he of all people has no peace, then who can have God's peace? I was perplexed.

After I had finished learning much of the Qur'an by heart, I spent more time in the Ahmadi mosque listening to the conversation of the elders. I wanted to know what made us of the Ahmadiyya community different from other Muslims. By this time, I had become well aware of the existence of such differences. In villages nearby where orthodox Muslims lived, my friends and I heard the epithets applied to Ahmadis:

"Get away from us, *Mirzai*! *Kafir*—Unbelievers! Pagans! Unclean!"

Not surprisingly, our lives were lived within our own community as far as possible. Within its accepted boundaries we were safe.

Our town, Rabwah, is situated northwest of Lahore, near a river. My father loved the river and enjoyed going there to fish. I sometimes think that this was his way of escaping the troubles he had! I would see him stride off in his long boots, wearing his loose-fitting brown clothes that would not show the dirt and dust, and he would be gone for hours. What did my father think about at such times? Did he have the doubts that even at my young age were beginning to trouble me? I never knew, for no Pakistani father would confide in his young son about such things.

When I was ten, I was sitting in the mosque one day listening as usual to the men talking with the teacher. The discussion turned to the power of prayer—something in which I was very interested. The noon prayer had just finished, and I heard one of the old people say, "If a person standing on the river bank has faith in the *Kalima*, he could cross the river as though on dry land." My heart beat faster. Could prayer really accomplish such a thing! Like all Muslims, I had known the *Kalima* from a very young age. Quietly I got up and slipped away from the assembly.

Once outside, I hurried to the river, a mile away. Standing breathlessly on the bank, I fixed my eyes on the water flowing silently past my feet. Some fishermen from a non-Ahmadi village were out in a boat, but they were far away from me. I looked around; no one else was in sight. In a loud voice, I repeated the sacred words of the *Kalima*: "In the name of Allah, the great and merciful, I believe that there is no God but God and that Muhammad is His Prophet."

I was wearing my grey school uniform of *shalwar* and *kamiz*, the long baggy shirt and trousers common to the Pathans and Punjabis. I wondered whether I should take my clothes off, then remembered that I had come to walk on the water, not to sink in it! However, I did take off my *chappals*, the open sandals on my feet.

With uncertain footsteps I put one foot into the water. My resolve faltered as I realized that it was not firm like the river bank, but desperately I surged forward into the river. The water rose to my knees. I thought that if I went a few steps further perhaps it would work and I would find myself walking on the water. Once more I said the *Kalima*, determinedly, willing it to work for me. I took another step, but all of a sudden the river bed fell away from me, and I could not stand. I slipped down into the water. Fear caught my throat. I could not swim! I knew that I would drown and cried out in desperation.

Oh, the joy of those strong arms under my shoulders! Somehow the fishermen had heard my cries and had come paddling up to save me. I was crying with embarrassment and anger when they hauled me into their boat. When I calmed down a little, one of them said to me, "Well, *baba*, that was a strange thing to do wasn't it? Why were you trying to swim in your clothes?" I began to cry again as I realized how close I had been to death. Also, I was afraid and decided that I had better tell them the truth. I dared not look at them as I confessed, "I am sorry, but I thought that if I said the *Kalima* with faith I would be able to walk on the water."

Even as I said it, it sounded so unlikely. What would these men think? They stared at me, amazed, then one of them threw back his head and laughed loudly and unkindly, "Oh, you child of a pagan. Your father is a pagan, your mother is a pagan, your whole family is Qadian? *Mirzai*. How can you, an unclean person, believe that God will hear you? Did you really think that you could recite the holy *Kalima* and cross the river dry-shod? Get out of here, you unbeliever, and tell your family to become Muslims and then come back here and try again! Run away, or I'll drown you!"

He looked so threatening that I was terrified. As soon as the boat drew alongside the bank, I twisted out of his grasp, scrambled ashore and ran towards the village. I was overcome with shame and, now that I had recovered from my fright, anger that God had not answered my prayer. I burned with the thought as I made my way home. My feet were sore, for I had lost my *chappals* during my unhappy experiment, and I feared the wrath of my father when it was found that they were missing. By this time, my clothes had dried out, but how could I explain the loss of my footwear? I felt lonely and afraid.

It was just as I had feared. My mother pounced on me as soon as I got home, "Where have you been? Why have you been away all this time?"

I could not answer her, and my mother beat me there and then. Later, when my father returned, she told him of my absence from home, and he, in turn, shouted at me. I still recall the shame I felt when, at the sound of his loud angry voice, I lost control of myself. The stain on my clothes was like a stain on my soul. So I told them the whole story. My sister and mother laughed when I spoke of trying to walk on water, but my father looked at me seriously when I said to him, crying, "But Daddy, we ... we are Muslim, aren't we? Why did he call us *kafir* – unbelievers, pagan's … Pagans were around in the Prophet Muhammad's time and the Qur'an says they vexed and troubled him. We are not like that! We believe the Qur'an, we say our prayers five times a day. Why did that man say we're pagan?"

I sobbed and my father watched me silently. Receiving no answer, I plucked up courage and said, "I want to know these things, Daddy. I have been reading about them and studying these things by myself."

My father seemed lost in thought, but at last he said, "You're too young for these things, Masood. When you grow up you'll come to understand these religious things. I can't talk with you now. Tomorrow I will speak with your teacher. Come along now; it's time for bed."

He did not speak unkindly, but all that night the only thing I could think about was that my father was going to complain to my teacher, Muhammad Ismail, and that he would beat me.

I was completely confused as I went to bed. I had always been an enquiring sort of boy and this incident upset me. The word *kafir* kept ringing in my ears, and I walked on sharp thorns of dread, thinking of the teacher's anger. I recited all the prayers and the passages of the Qur'an that I knew by heart, but my main feeling was not fear, it was anger—at Allah! Why had he failed me? Why did he not answer my prayer?

Had I been deceived?

"O Allah," I said scornfully to him, "can't you understand any language except Arabic? Is that why you do not hear a prayer in Urdu or Pashtu? Is that why you did not understand what I was trying to do? Or did you not want to hear me? Are you angry with me as my parents are?" I turned my face to the wall and wept for the lost dreams of childhood.

That night is when I dreamed I came to the cross-road. I was lost and my Father put his arms around me and reassured me and brought me back to my home....

Until 1972, when all Ahmadi schools and colleges were nationalized and brought into the Pakistani school system, Ahmadis would prefer to attend only the educational institutions run by the Ahmadiyya movement. It was to an Ahmadi school that I went as a child. I enjoyed school and I greatly respected Mirza Muhammad Ismail, my teacher.

Muhammad Ismail was an old man with a long white beard. Most Ahmadis had short trimmed beards, as did my father, but Muhammad Ismail's beard reached right down his chest. He was rather frail, but he had the reputation of being a scholar in Rabwah, because of the many books he owned. He was a learned man with a vast knowledge of Islam. He must have found his young pupils quite a trial at times.

The day after I had tried to walk on the river I was back in my place in the schoolroom, feeling very afraid and apprehensive. What had my father reported to Muhammad Ismail? As usual, our teacher called the roll, and when he had checked that all the pupils were present, he called me to the front of the class. "Masood, I have received a complaint from your father. You must tell your parents wherever you go, young man. If you had been drowned, what would they think? Do be careful next time."

With that, he dismissed me. I stuttered my thanks respectfully, but continued to stand in front of him, wanting to tell him of my dream. Finally he said, "What is it, Masood?"

"Sir," I replied, "I had a dream ... last night...."

He looked at me thoughtfully.

"A dream?" Then softly, as though to himself, "So you too."

I felt a tingling of elation. So he had had a dream! The old man had spoken to him! Could it be possible that … ? But he was speaking to me again, "What was it you saw, my son?"

He led me out of earshot of the class, and I told him my dream. He fell into deep thought and then said simply, "Masood, do not say anything to anyone of this. Do you understand?"

I nodded in obedience, my heart singing. Somehow, though I could not understand it, it seemed that Allah did care. Despite yesterday's fiasco, despite the beating and the tears, he was there, he cared.

_____ 3 _____

Growing Up

My parents were fighting again! I heard my mother's raised voice, and I wanted to screw my fingers into my ears to block out the shameful things she was saying to my father. As was so often the case, she was reproaching him for going out and staying away for days at a time. Rumors had reached her that my father was going to another city and seeing other women. Not for the first time I reflected that to have more than one wife was a burden I never wanted to bear.

I thought of my friend Sayeed. His home was so much more peaceful than ours. His parents did not fight as mine did. His parents had money to buy him nice clothes and other things that mine could not afford for me or my sister, Jamila, or my brother, Mahmood. I did not even know all my father's children by his other wives, and it seemed to me that there must be a better way than this for families to live. It was odd, but it seemed that Muhammad, our Prophet, had the same sort of trouble that my father did! Though Islam gives privileges to wives, it seems that there is no way that human jealousy can tolerate the special attention that one wife receives at the expense of another.

And there was never enough money. I knew that my mother had some money and received a little occasionally from her father in Tarnab, but still it was difficult to live. In any case, my father would always manage to spend whatever we had. He was very fond of his friends and would spend money on entertaining them whether we could afford it or not. My mother once became so angry with my father that she hit him on the head with a bicycle pump as they argued on the veranda, and my father fell down as if unconscious for a few moments. I cried out to my mother, "*Ammi*, please don't hit Father. Please don't quarrel. What will the neighbors think?"

I am ashamed now to think that I was more concerned with our reputation in the community than with my father. But my father, furiously angry, struggled to his feet, "You shut up! Keep your face out of this. It's our problem, not yours."

My face was red as I fled from the veranda. Perhaps I was too sensitive, but I always used to fancy that my mother cared more for my sister, Jamila, than she did for me. Mother used to teach Jamila Urdu, as she did not go to school with me, and they were very close. My mother rarely showed me affection and I longed for it. Perhaps she was afraid that I would become like my father, and in any case Mother was naturally closer to her daughter.

It worried me that Mother didn't have enough food for us. Once I heard her say to my father as I passed their room, "We have no food in the house; I need five rupees for rice and *dhal*. I can't feed the children on what you give me."

Father gave her some money, reluctantly, but it cannot have been enough for she beat us children, proclaiming:

"As your father is, so will you be."

Of course, Mother must have been under a great strain. I felt that I just had to help. I began to get little jobs that would help me bring in some money. I was able to wash some dishes in a small restaurant, and later I helped a fruit seller in the bazaar, washing his fruit and helping display them. Mother was surprised when I brought her the money, and I think she was pleased, but she did not say much.

And all the time I was learning more of prayer. It seems to me now that God had put a special desire in my heart to pray. Even when my relationship with my family was at its worst, I did not stop praying, and God honoured that desire.

One day, in 1963, after my parents had quarreled, I suddenly remembered that I needed a new exercise book for arithmetic the next day, my present one being full. "What can I do," I asked myself, "for Daddy's angry now. How can I ask him for another book?" Instinctively, I prayed, "O Allah, turn my father's anger to peace so I can go to him and ask for some money to buy an exercise book."

Alas, it did not happen. My father left home, still angry.

I am ashamed to say that I stole some sheets of paper from a boy's book at school that day. For a while these were enough, but by the time I had done almost all my sums, the paper was finished. I went to the next room where my mother was teaching Jamila. I asked for some money, but she did not hear me, and I felt that to insist would make her angry.

In desperation, I searched for my sister's bag, but she had hidden it, knowing that I needed paper! I was so scared of not having my homework finished that I resolved to wait up until my father came home. I settled down to read a story book. And then I slept....

About a minute later, so it seemed, I was shaken roughly, and I heard my mother's angry voice, "Here it is one o'clock in the morning, and you're sleeping over your books with the lights still on! Your father couldn't get an education, and now it seems you won't either! Get up you lazy boy and get into bed." She turned off the lights and stamped out.

Next morning my first thought was for my unfinished homework. I used to walk the mile to school each day, and that day as I went I prayed, rather selfishly, "O God, let the teacher be sick today!"

But then I realized that still meant he would be back at work the following day, so I prayed again, "O God, I want to find a rupee on the way to school so I can buy two exercise books, a pencil and an eraser at the school bookstall."

My faith was strong, and I checked the ground carefully, sure that I would find my heart's desire. About halfway to school, I decided that perhaps my expectations had been too great and prayed yet again, "Well, God, if one rupee is too much then a fifty-paisa coin (half a rupee) will do!"

The school gate came into view, and I reduced my request to twenty-five paisa, and then just ten paise for some pages to paste into my book. But the ground was bare of any coins, and greatly discouraged, I walked on towards the gate and the bookstall that stood close by. Just then I heard a familiar voice say, "Son, my child." My heart leapt. I knew this voice. Instantly I turned and saw the white-robed old man of my dream. I began to tremble from surprise and fear. As if from a great distance I heard his voice again, "Son, don't be a coward.

Take this rupee. Buy your things and finish your home-work. There's still time before the bell is rung."

The voice faded, and as though in a trance I heard the bookstall owner say to me, "Well now, what do you need?"

I was utterly surprised and confused. I was standing at the bookstall, and a rupee coin was in my hand. I managed to give my order to the man and sat down on a nearby bench to complete my homework. Just as I finished, the bell rang for class.

When the teacher asked us a few minutes later whether we had completed our homework, my glad cry of "Yes!" was gladder and louder than all the others!

I was thirteen when I completed seventh grade. About this time I became friendly with a student called Ahmed who was in the ninth grade. He was a quiet sort of boy and had a bent towards spiritual things. I was glad to be his friend. He was very tall, towering above me. Because he was older and knew much more than I did, he helped me in my studies.

Ahmed's father was an Ahmadi missionary. The Ahmadiyya sect has always been very missionary minded, and because of this, has spread the teachings of Mirza Ghulam Ahmad throughout the world. Ahmed's father also taught in the Ahmadiyya missionary training college in Rabwah and was known as a good teacher and preacher. I loved to visit their home and they were always kind to me.

One day in the cool winter season, I went to see Ahmed at his home. We played together, and while we were playing I heard some sweet singing. At first I thought it was the radio, but Ahmed said, "No, that's the sweepers singing. Come on, let's go and see them."

He took me by the hand and we climbed the stairs to the flat roof. Ahmed's house adjoined a colony of smaller houses, and from where we stood we could see into the courtyards of these houses. In one of them men, women and children were sitting and singing. Our shadows fell on the flagstones of the courtyard, and some of the people looked up to see us standing there. We watched them without moving. I did not know it then, but these were the first Christian songs I ever heard.

A man stood up, bowed his head and started talking to the group. They listened intently to his words, but we were too far away to hear what he said. Nevertheless, I found the scene below us very interesting. Finally, I felt Ahmed's hand on my arm, "Come on, Masood. Mummy's calling us. Let's go down."

Ahmed's mother made us some tea and then Ahmed said to me, "Come, I want to show you my library." Ahmed was very fond of his books. I loved books too, and was proud of my small collection of boys' stories. I used to buy them when I had some extra pocket money, or some money from odd jobs I had done for neighbors. Like Ahmed, I also bought books about prophets and other Muslim heroes. Among Ahmed's books and magazines I suddenly saw a small book entitled *The Gospel of John*. The title sounded interesting, and I thought at first that it must be a book for children. The Urdu word for gospel, *Injil*, reminded me that this must be one of the Holy Books. I knew this because we used to read and memorize in our 'Islamic Studies' period.

The Holy Books are four: The *Torah* given to Moses, The *Zabur* (psalms) given to David, The *Injil* (gospel) given to Jesus, The Holy Qur'an given to Muhammad.

"If this is the *Injil* given to Jesus the Prophet," I asked Ahmed, "why is it written in Urdu and not in Arabic, our holy language?"

Ahmed's mother came in before he could reply to my question and said to me, irritably, "Child, those sweepers gave him this book. I told the boy not to keep it, but he lied and said he'd given it back to them. Here, give it to me, and I'll burn it now."

I was horrified. "No, Auntie," I said urgently (this term is often used when speaking to our friends' mothers). "Please let me have it." Ahmed chimed in, "Yes, Mother, let him have it; he has very little to read."

Ahmed's mother relented. "All right, but I don't want to see that book in this house again."

Soon after, I said goodbye to Ahmed and left with an armful of his magazines and my new treasure, the *Injil*.

When I arrived home, Jamila was playing with her friends. Perhaps they were bored with their usual girls' games with Jamila's dolls, but when they saw me with the magazines, they snatched them out of my hand, and the little gospel dropped to the ground. I felt very angry with my sister and would have slapped her for dropping the Holy Book of the Prophet Jesus, but my mother was sitting nearby, sewing, and my hand dropped. I picked up the book and hurried to my room to read it.

The reading of that book opened a whole new world for me that evening. I finished reading it before I slept, and my mind whirled with the new ideas with which it challenged me. Was Jesus really the Christ, that is the Messiah? I well knew that the Qadiani Ahmadis believed that Mirza Ghulam Ahmad was the Messiah. I knew from my reading that the Prophet Jesus was called the Kalima—the Word, or the Logos. He was ruh'Allah— the Spirit of God. The Qur'an also calls him Son of Mary (never, of course, of God) and also Isa.

I knew that the Qur'an taught that Jesus performed miracles. Sayeed, my neighbor and schoolmate, had a series of little books on the Holy Prophets, and one of these was about the Prophet Isa, or Jesus. Now, I thought to myself, I must borrow that book from Sayeed again and compare the two.

The next day was Friday, and this being the holy day for all Muslims, school was closed. I borrowed the book from Sayeed and spent most of the day comparing the two accounts. There were many differences between them.

I was deep in thought as I made my way to the Central Grand Mosque for Friday prayers. I noticed Muhammad Ismail, my old teacher, among the worshippers, and when he saw me he smiled, happy to see me praying. I knew that he had hopes that I would one day become an Ahmadiyya missionary and carry the teachings of our Prophet throughout the world. After the prayers he fell in beside me, and we walked home companionably together. It occurred to me that he might be able to answer some of my questions.

"Sir?" I began, rather nervously.

"What is it, Masood? Do you want to ask me something?"

I nodded and said hesitantly, "Sir, is God our Father and are we his sons?"

He stopped walking and looked at me, sternly I thought. "Who on earth told you that?" he asked, amazed.

"I read it in the *Injil*," I said simply.

"The *Injil*? Where did you get that, young man?" he asked me. "Who gave it to you? Where is it now?"

I was rather afraid of his questions, but managed to say, "I got it from Ahmed and it's at my home."

He began to walk on, rather faster this time, and said, "I think you had better come home with me, Masood, and I will try to answer your questions for you."

I hurried along beside him, sure that now I would get some answers.

At his home, he made me sit down and went to another room to fetch some books. His wife came in, and I stood up politely and said, "Asalamu alaikum. Peace be upon you."

She smiled at me and kissed me. "And what is your name?" she asked. "Are you one of my husband's pupils?" As I answered her, my old teacher came in with his arms full of books.

"Will you please make tea for us?" he said to his wife. "We'll need it, for this young man asks deep questions for one so young!"

His wife smiled at me affectionately, "Children like this one can spread our news to the end of the world." I was to remember her words much later. ...

While we were waiting for our tea, he took up a large, black book and opened it.

"This is the Bible of the Christians," he said. "In it we find the Torah, the Zabur and the *Injil*—the law, the psalms and the gospel."

I took it from his hands and turned the pages with great interest. He turned to the gospel of John, and I noticed that it was the last of four such gospels—all *Injil*s! I asked him about this, curious.

"No, Masood, there are not four different *Injil*s. It is one book but in four parts, because four different people wrote it."

My teacher told me many things that afternoon, most of which I have forgotten, but I well remember him saying, at some point, "We Muslims believe that the Torah, the Zabur and the *Injil* are the Holy Heavenly Books, but they are incomplete without the Qur'an. The first three books, as written in the Bible by the Christians, have been perverted and distorted from their original purity. There was only one *Injil*, but now there are four parts. There are other true revelations, too, but the Christians do not mention these. As these books are now," and he solemnly tapped the Bible he held, "they lead to confusion. There is only one God. As our Qur'an says, 'Say: He is Allah, the One! Allah, the eternally Besought of all! He begetteth not, nor was begotten. There is none comparable to Him.' How can we say then that God is our Father and we are his sons when He says of Himself, 'He begetteth not, nor is begotten'?"

Slowly, I nodded my head. Before I left, I asked him, "Sir, is there not a story about Jesus walking on water?" Even three years later the memory of my own attempt was still fresh in my mind!

My teacher answered me kindly, "There is indeed my son, but His power to do miracles was given to prophets and apostles, and you are neither apostle nor prophet. Even a simple faith requires a mature mind."

He walked me home, and standing at the gate in the gathering dusk, I promised to give him the gospel of John I had and never to think about false things again.

_____ 4 _____

Preparing for Him

Two years went by, and I was fifteen. At home, things became worse and worse. My father's financial position was now rather shaky, it seemed, and my parents were always arguing about something. It made us children very unhappy.

My thirst to learn had not abated, but the shortage of money at home made it difficult to keep up with school fees. Because of this, I undertook more and more odd jobs for my neighbors in return for their paying my school fees. I would spend time each evening washing clothes, cleaning and doing the shopping.

At this time God seemed very close. I realize now that I never thought of Him as the impersonal, far-away God that Islam teaches, but I really prayed expecting God to hear and answer me by solving my personal problems. I had few real friends, and perhaps because of this I turned to God all the more.

I also came to enjoy fishing, as my father did. I did not usually go with him but would go by myself to the river. On some occasions, I am sorry to say, I took his equipment without his permission.

During these times at the river bank I would talk to God. Once I prayed, "O God, today please give me two or three fish. You know that I want them for my family, for their food."

The rod jumped in my hand, and an enormous fish broke the surface of the water! I caught my breath as I was almost pulled into the river. I was afraid that the line would break, and that would be a bigger disaster than losing this great fish, for it was my father's line, and I knew he would not easily forgive me. Fortunately, help was at hand. Someone saw the struggle I was having with the fish and rushed over to help. Between us, we managed to bring a ten-pound fish to shore. It was the biggest fish I had ever caught, and I felt full of awe at the answer to my prayer. However, it never occurred to me to put things right with my father, to confess that I had taken his rod without permission.

In my heart I was full of questions. I could not understand why the Ahmadi people had nothing to do with other Muslims, such as those from across the river in Chiniot. Our lives seemed very tedious, and like many a youth, I was feeling more and more rebellious. I was proud of the questions I asked the elders and happy when they could not answer me satisfactorily. For a while I did not so much want to find out the truth as to defeat others in argument. To this end, I spent long hours in my books "conducting my research," as I called it to anyone who asked!

Ahmadis are proud of their strict moral code. Like all good Muslims, they are strongly opposed to the use of alcohol, and even tobacco, and have strict penalties for those who indulge. Of course, there were always some who used it secretly, but openly, never.

There was no television in our town in those days and no cinemas that were permitted to show commercial films. We were allowed to see films with an Ahmadi,

Muslim or religious theme, and religious dramas were very popular. But the youths of Rabwah longed to learn more of the outside world, and I was no different. Some of my friends once dared to visit the cinema in Chiniot, five miles away, but they were caught and beaten severely. The Ahmadiyya Community Centre, the *Amoor-i-Ama*, maintained its own disciplinary force to deal with problems in the Ahmadi community, partly to keep such matters out of the hands of the police. This force was known as the *Mujahed*, and from the age of twelve or so, every boy would receive some training from this body.

I was to learn to my cost, much later, how effective this force was!

My parents insisted that I did not leave Rabwah, though I was intensely curious to see how the other Muslims lived. I longed to talk with them and to dispute with them. No matter how I pleaded, however, my parents remained firm, and I rebelled.

I visited the cinema twice in Chiniot, with my friends. Chiniot was like another world, and the cinema was luxury to me. The films I saw transported me away from my problems as I identified with their characters. The films glorified our Pakistani nation, portraying the heroes as noble and patriotic men who would even give up their lives for their country's well-being. I was deeply moved and stirred by their sacrifice. By contrast, the ones opposing them were grasping people, only concerned with their own wealth and happiness. Since the memory of the British colonial regime was still fresh in the mind of the nation, I suppose it is not strange that the "enemy" was often shown as British! How was it, I wondered, that anyone could be so cruel!

I escaped a beating once, when the so-called friends with whom I had gone to Chiniot reported me to the *Amoor-i-Ama*. When the matter came to the ears of the Ahmadi teachers, they could not believe that I had gone to Chiniot just to visit the cinema.

"It can't be," they said. "If Masood went, it must have been to debate with some Muslim men there."

They would not believe the truth about me, and of course, this was not good for my pride! Despite all these things, God never seemed far away.

One day, my father gave me two rupees to go to the bazaar to buy cooking oil. I clutched the money tightly in my hand and ran to the *til* oil shop. On the way I noticed a small crowd of people gathered round a man who had a trained monkey. The monkey was doing all sorts of tricks and antics, and I watched, fascinated. To this day, I don't know how it happened, but when I finally tore myself away the two rupees were no longer in my hand! I felt quite devastated and cried out to God, "O God, give me back the money"

I wept all the way home, for the shopkeeper would not give me the oil without the money to pay for it. I turned in at the gate of our house, knowing that I would be beaten, and there, lying at the door, was the money. Two silver coins glinted in the sunlight! How they came to be there I cannot tell. There may be some simple explanation, but to me it was a miracle. Once more, God had answered prayer.

Meanwhile, I was working for Sayeed's family in the evenings. However, my relationship with Sayeed himself had deteriorated badly. His father was always away overseas, and his older brother was a strong influence on him. He was a violent person with a bad reputation in our community. Sayeed seemed to resent my wanting to study so much, for he was not very good at school work. He began to tease me. In games he would throw the ball to hit me deliberately and would taunt me, "Come on servant boy! Bring me my books. Quickly now!"

I dared not retaliate, because I knew that if his parents stopped paying my school fees, I would lose my education. But it was hard to be quiet.

Sayeed went too far one day. He tore out the pages of my exercise book, where I had done my homework, just before the teacher checked it. When I opened my book to show the teacher my work, the pages were not there. Sayeed had already shown his homework, but he had pretended that my work was his. The teacher checked when he saw that my work had been torn out, and Sayeed was discovered and punished. Humiliated, he beat me after school that day. I was very discouraged.

The time of the *Eid-ul-adha* (Festival of Sacrifice) approached, and I was looking forward to it. Coming after Ramadan, this is one of the major festivals in the Islamic year. It commemorates that time when Ishmael, the son of Abraham, was to have been sacrificed. What is taught in the Torah of the Jews, of course, is that God provided a lamb for the sacrifice in place of Isaac (Genesis 22), but Muslims teach that it was Ishmael in place of whom God provided the lamb. Although relating the story of the sacrifice in Sura 37, the Qur'an itself does not mention the name of Ishmael.

On the festival day, Sayeed's mother called me to her home. I went gladly, thinking that perhaps she might give me some *eidi,* or festival money, to mark the occasion. She had already given me some of Sayeed's clothes for the festival and I was wearing these as I went to her house. She sent me to buy some things she needed from the bazaar. When I returned she was in the kitchen. Sayeed was there too, and as I came in, he pulled my arm roughly and cried, "Get out of my clothes!" His mother angrily rebuked him, saying that she had given them to me, but he did not listen. She ordered him out of the kitchen, and he went, but with very bad grace.

She gave me a gift of a few rupees, telling me to give them to my mother, but that I might keep one of them for myself. She also gave me a stainless steel pot full of cooked rice to take to my mother. I thanked her and left, carrying the pot.

On the way home, I saw Sayeed and a friend of his ahead. I tried to go past, but they grabbed the pot, and in the struggle for possession of it, it fell to the ground, spilling the rice. I was close to tears. Sayeed and the other boy tugged at my clothes, and tried to pull them off. I tried my best to escape, but they held me fast. "Look at the servant boy," Sayeed hissed spitefully, "wearing clothes that don't belong to him."

He lunged at me, trying to grab my belt, and I stooped to pick up the pot and hit him in the face. With a cry of rage he fell down, and I hit the other boy too! As he staggered, I fled for my home.

During the fracas I lost the money the kind woman had given me, and as always, afraid, I hid in the toilet. Soon afterwards, I heard knocking at the front door as the neighbors came to tell my parents what had happened. My father was at home, and in a moment he came through to the toilet and called, "Masood, come out at once. Do you hear me? Come out!"

I came out trembling, and at once he began to beat me with his hand and dragged me to the people outside. Furiously, he said, "Here, take this worthless brat and kill him! We don't need him."

My heart failed me at his terrible words. I had never known him so angry, and I wanted to die. In front of me the enraged face of Sayeed's elder brother appeared, and he started to kick me. I fell to the ground to cover my face, but his boots kept striking me. At last, someone pulled him off, and I felt a man drag me to my feet.

"Get out of here," he ordered me.

Stumbling, I ran. I don't know how long I ran, but my feet took me to the river where I sat on a rock, almost too tired to think. My whole body seemed to be one bruise, and my ribs ached painfully. I wept as I sat there and shook my fist at God.

"Allah! Why didn't you save me from this? Are you so cruel and heartless? I didn't ask to be born into a home where no one cares for me or loves me, and now you, too, have forsaken me. Yes, you of all, have forsaken me. From today I am not going to talk to you anymore. I will be silent. I called you so many times, but you did not listen. Today I was beaten unfairly, and you did not say one word in my defense."

I stood up on that big rock with an effort and shouted at God, "Allah, you are cruel. You are a cruel king. If you really are the Beneficent and Merciful then talk to me. Today, on this Eid Festival day I have been kicked out of my home. You are an evil God. You are not good, but evil. If you are like this, then why don't you just kill us? Why do you keep us suffering like this? Answer me, O God. I must have an answer!"

I walked away from the rock and in desperation began to strike my head against a stone wall nearby.

With a searing flash, lightning tore the sky apart! I looked up, and black clouds appeared, and I heard a roar of thunder. Seconds later the sky opened above me, and the rain pelted down, soaking me to the skin.

I quailed inwardly, thinking of Noah's Flood! Fear gripped me as I remembered my own words, "Why don't you kill us? Why do you keep us suffering?" Did God really intend to kill me? I could not say as I cowered there under a huge rock, trying to keep out of the torrential rain, but I knew that I did not want to die.

A bolt of lightning struck the ground nearby, and I cried out! I looked at the place, sure that the next thing it struck would be me, but all I saw was a small fire in a bush. Briefly it flared up, then the flame died, and a wisp of smoke showed against the rain. Seeing this, I remembered the incident in the Qur'an about the Prophet Moses. He had seen a fire in a bush, too. I was fearful and felt unclean. Surely God was here and was watching me. I began to pray aloud for His forgiveness.

Gradually, the rain eased, and I crept out from underneath my rock and went across to look at the bush. I stepped forward fearfully, but all I could see was a burnt bush. Foolishly, I thought that perhaps God's presence had been there when I challenged Him. Again I looked at the bush, but it was burnt and silent. At that moment the lightning briefly flashed again, and I fell forward on my face in the mud.

"No, no, God! Please forgive me!"

I was sure that I would be struck dead the next instant.

I was not, however, and cautiously I raised my head. There was nothing there. No more rain fell, and I stood up and began to walk back towards the village. Several times I looked back, but I could see nothing unusual.

For a long time I wandered, but eventually found myself back in Rabwah. I heard the *adhan,* the call to prayer, coming from the mosque. It was noon and time for *Zuhr*, so I joined the crowd of people going to the mosque. Some looked at me curiously for I was very dirty. I went to the wash basin provided at the mosque for ceremonial purification before prayer. I managed to get the mud off my *chappals* and the worst of the dirt from my clothes. I slipped quietly into the row to join in the prayers.

After I had prayed, a man came forward and took me angrily by the ear and half dragged me out of the mosque. He slapped me and said, "If you want to pray here, young man, you first go and repair your trousers and then come and pray."

He pushed me away, and I flushed red with shame. During the time at the river, I had slipped when I was trying to escape in the rain; it must have been then that my trousers had torn at the back. I was very embarrassed and ashamed. I walked home gingerly, afraid that people might notice the tear.

When I got home, the door was shut. I did not have the courage to open it or knock. I was hungry, and that reminded me of the spilt rice and the money that I had lost in the morning. I went back to the place where Sayeed had fought with me; though I did not find the money, the rice was still there. I looked around, but no one was in sight, so I took a handful of the rice and slipped it into my pocket. I ate some of it as I looked around quickly, but the taste of the sand mixed with the rice was very unpleasant. However, I was hungry and eventually ate it all.

After I had finished, I thought it would be good to visit Ahmed, my friend. Besides, I had not yet greeted his family on this *Eid* Festival occasion, as custom demanded. It occurred to me that I might get something to eat too and perhaps borrow a needle and thread to mend my trousers.

When I reached Ahmed's home, there was a lock on the door. I waited disconsolately, but no one came. I wandered down the back street, just to fill in time and found myself on the street where the Christian sweepers lived. Their houses were just hovels made of mud bricks, not the solid stone that Ahmadi families used. These sweepers were people of low-caste Hindu background and had originally become Christian many years before when Hinduism seemed to offer them no chance to better themselves. They were obliged to do only the most menial tasks, such as cleaning toilets, and many of them seemed to know little of what Christianity really involves. However, as I was to find, there were some very fine believers among them. No Ahmadi would have anything to do with them, except out of necessity, and I felt strange as I stood there, listening to their children playing happily together.

I was attracted by the sound of sweet singing, as I had been two years before. I walked towards the house from where the sound came and found the door wide open. Inside, about twenty men, women and children were sitting on the floor and singing a song about the Prophet Jesus. One man sat in front of them. He had a book in his hand, and I recognized it as the Bible, the book I had seen in Muhammad Ismail's house.

Several of the people now turned and noticed me standing there. Smiling, they beckoned me to come in, their fingers bent downwards as we do in Pakistan. I hesitated, but eventually went in and sat down with the men on the mats. I was conscious of my torn trousers and took care to sit in such a way that no one would notice. The group sang a final song, and after prayer, began to get up to go. The man next to me smiled at me and said, "It is finished."

I also stood up to leave, and one of the women whispered something to the man with the Bible and gestured towards me. The man said something to her, then came over to me. Putting his hand on my shoulder he said, "Son, who are you, and where do you come from?"

I told him that I had come to visit my friend who lived nearby, but that as he was not at home I had made my way further down the road and had come across the group.

Somebody came with a cup of tea for the pastor, and he courteously invited me to join him. I sat beside him on the *charpai,* the rope bed, and we began to talk together. After a while, I noticed that only I, the pastor and the family were left. All the others had gone. "Sir," I began diffidently, "where can I get a Bible like you have?"

He looked at me honestly. "It's not difficult" he said, "but your parents and your Ahmadiyya community will not let you read it."

"I will read it," I replied, "even if I have to read it secretly."

At that, he pulled a small book out of a bag beside him on the bed.

"Here, take this. It's the New Testament. Read it, and when you have finished it, I'll give you the full Bible."

I thanked him and took it, feeling unaccountably glad.

He pushed my cup of tea towards me, "Drink it. The tea will be cold if you don't finish it now."

I swallowed the sweet milky tea, thinking that this was the first time I had ever had the opportunity to eat with these people of another community. Usually, self-respecting Muslims would never eat with low-caste

Christians. I was hungry and had a headache from the long day. The tea tasted good to me, even as I thought about the strangeness of my being with these people who believed that the Prophet Jesus was the Son of God. Without stopping to think, I blurted out, "Sir, why do you people believe that Jesus is the Son of God, since God has no wife and so cannot have children?" The man smiled and asked my name.

"Masood Ahmad Khan," I told him, wondering what he meant.

"Well, Masood, if I say to you, 'Son, come and do this job for me,' do you actually become my son because I called you Son? Do I thus become your father?' I shook my head, beginning to see what he meant. "Well," he continued, "it's the same with Jesus. He is a spiritual Son, and God is the Father.'

The way he said it, it seemed very simple to me. At this point the pastor stood up and said that he had to go, but that he would come again to the group the following month. We said goodbye, and I walked back to Ahmed's house, deep in thought. It was still locked for they had not come home. It was getting dark, and my body was aching. I was very cold for the rain had begun again. I touched the little New Testament under my shirt and sat hugging my knees trying to keep warm. Without realizing it, I slipped into unconsciousness.

When I came to my senses I was at home in my own bed! Ahmed's father was standing with my father beside my bed. Clearly he had brought me home, and my father thanked him, all the while standing with his hand placed affectionately on my head. Ahmed's father patted my arm, and after advising me kindly not to wander in the rain again, he left. As he walked out of the door, I felt my heart miss a beat! Where was my New Testament? I felt under my shirt for it, but it was not there. I was wearing dry clothes, so someone must have found the book. I looked carefully at my father's face. Did he know? Would he beat me again? At this moment, my mother came in with a cup of tea and a couple of aspirins for me. Tea is regarded by our people as the best medicine for colds and headaches, and it certainly tasted very good to me then.

I sipped the tea, and there beside my father on my table was the little Gideon New Testament that the pastor had given me. My father noticed me looking at it and picked it up. To my surprise, he handed it to me saying, "If you read this as a story, Masood, it's all right. But if you think too much about it and collect questions from it to argue about, then it will destroy your mind. God has given you wisdom and a thirst for knowledge.

If you want to be helped then come and talk to me. There's only one year of school left for you, and I think that after that you should be admitted to *Jami' Ahmadiyya* (Ahmadi Missionary College) here in Rabwah and become a missionary. I, and others also, feel you should do this once you have your school certificate."

This was a long speech for my father who hardly ever spoke to me except in anger, but he had still not finished. He went on, "When you're at college, son, you can learn all the doctrine you want. You will learn what we Ahmadis believe and what the people of Islam say. You can study the teaching of those who call us pagans and also that of the Christians. You will find out what all religions teach about God. You are not a child any longer, I'm sorry that I've hurt you. You always seem to be studying, and I've not been happy about it, it's true. I've not been able to afford your education."

He stood up, and sighed deeply.

"It's true that my marriages have not brought me happiness. I have been afraid that as my first wife and children left me through the door of death, so you too would leave me, Masood. I couldn't bear that. I knew too that those children who fought with you today were in the wrong, but what could I do?"

I was too surprised to speak. What strange things my father was saying. I wondered what I should say to him, but my mother stood up, annoyed, and said, "This is not the time for a lecture." She waved her hand scornfully at my father. "You should be in bed yourself. Come back some other time with your glue and paste to patch up your relationship with your son. My father's face was red as he walked out, but he did not say anything more then. My mother went after him, leaving me alone, and for a long time I heard the familiar, harsh words coming from the other room.

I opened the little book at random and read many pages, but when I heard footsteps outside my room I quickly slid the New Testament under my pillow and pretended to be asleep. Mother came in and saw me sleeping, as she thought; she turned off the lights and left. I slept soundly through the night.

When I awoke in the morning it was late. Imagine my joy at seeing Ahmed and his mother by my bed, anxious to know how I was. Seeing them I wanted to get up, but they would not permit it. We talked for a little while, and when my mother left to bring me a drink, Ahmed's mother gave me twenty rupees. It was a lot of money! I hesitated to accept it, but she quickly said, "Take it for your books, child. It's *eidi* for you. Hide it or your mother will see it."

Gratefully, I thanked her and put her money under my pillow. Then she went out to chat with my mother, leaving Ahmed with me.

My friend sat on the bed and I reached under the pillow saying, "Here, I want to show you something, brother."

I gave him the New Testament. He took one look at it and gave it back to me.

"But what's the matter? Read it."

Ahmed shook his head, "No, Masood. I will not read it. I'm not quite mad yet, and I don't want to become mad either."

"What are you saying, Ahmed?" I asked.

"I have read much of this book, brother, and my father has proved to me that it's perverted. Christianity is not a true religion, nor is that so-called Islam that labels us Ahmadis pagan. Their doctrine proves them to be *kafir* (pagan), not us. Because they do not believe in the *Masih-Maood* (Mirza Ghulam Ahmad), they condemn themselves."

I looked at him in amazement, for this was a new Ahmed who spoke to me. Since he had taken up his studies at Jami' Ahmadiyya and was hoping to follow in his father's footsteps, he had become much more opposed to ideas that did not agree with Ahmadiyya doctrines.

He talked for a few minutes about the Ahmadi "proofs" against the Christian and even against the majority position, and then his mother called him, and they had to leave. I watched him go with a tug in my heart. God seemed to be saying something to me, and I was not sure that it was something with which Ahmed would agree. Nevertheless, I felt a bond with this tall serious friend of my youth, and I knew that his parents loved me.

I tossed on my bed, unable to sleep. The darkness seemed to block out every attempt at clear thought. The night was oppressive, and I felt an unaccountable weight upon me. I heard again in my mind my mother's tearful accusations about me to my father.

"Oh God, my life is spoiled," she had wailed. "I am to be held in disrepute in this town because of my silly son who goes to listen to non-Ahmadies and the Christians. My son! That he should become a worshipper of idols and a *kafir* (unbeliever). He goes to these people who are against us and against the truth. My own son! He will become some crazy preacher, or even become like you."

For the twentieth time I turned on my bed and tried to sleep, but sleep eluded me. Could I separate myself from these Ahmadi people, I asked myself, and if I did, then what? After all, I was one of them. I could not imagine what my religion would be. What kind of doctrine would I embrace? It seemed that a voice whispered to my soul, and it said—Islam!

Islam! Which Islam? That of the Sunnis? The Shi'ites? Which one of Islam's more than eighty sects and numerous denominations would you follow? And again the darkness seemed like a solid wall.

Was it true, what they said of the Christians? Did they worship three gods, when all believers knew that there was only one God, the true God: Allah the Merciful, the Beneficent and Muhammad is ... Well, isn't he? Is he not the true Prophet of God? I groaned inwardly. The weight on my chest seemed to grow heavier. My mind was whirling in confusion. I felt as though some evil people, or forces, or spirits were laughing at me and that they were grabbing me and boxing me with their fists. I was sweating with fear and loathing.

All of a sudden I remembered the gospel, something I had read about rebuking evil spirits. I tried to cry out, but again that mocking laughter seemed to fill the room. I felt that evil things were trying to bite me, and I was paralyzed by the weight of my body. I cried out, "O Creator of the universe, help me, save me. O the True God! Please help me."

The habit of childhood stood by me, and I recited three *suras* (chapters) of the Qur'an in quick succession. And again I cried out to God. Again I thought of Jesus rebuking the spirits, and even as I had the thought the weight left me; the heavy thing moved from my chest, and there was only calm and peace in the room. Despite my earlier fears I got up and went for a drink of water and thought of Jesus! Soon I slept, and all was peace and security.

_____ 5 _____

Pressing on to the Truth

I spent more and more time in study. To be frank, much of my study was aimed at finding questions that the Ahmadi teachers could not answer. I compared Islam and Christianity and studied the lives of the prophets. Even in school, I bored my classmates with my questions, and there was scarcely an hour when I did not think about these things. I can see now that God was planting in me a great hunger for the truth, but as yet I did not recognize it. I knew only that I had to study, and as I studied that desire for real truth grew in my soul.

However, my search for truth faced three obstacles: the Ahmadis, the orthodox Muslims and the Christians. First, there were the Ahmadiyya doctrines of my father's Qadiani party with its absolute insistence that Mirza Ghulam Ahmad was the Messiah and Mahdi, the promised one. Clearly this did not please the orthodox Muslims who insisted that we were pagans and worse. And as for the Christians—they were so far from my way of thinking, and I had had no experience of them really. I knew only that there was an attraction about them, though they were so different.

Whenever I faced a problem, I would try to find out what all three groups said about it. By 1967 I was a member of the *Itfal ul Ahmadiyya,* or Children of the Ahmadis, and was supposed to become a member of the older group known as *Khudam ul Ahmadiyya,* the Servants of the Ahmadis. I knew that these groups completely disapproved of my studies. At the same time, I felt a little exasperated with the elders of the mosque and Islamic Studies teachers at school, for they saw all my questions as bad! It seemed to me that if they were so sure about their beliefs, then they should welcome the opportunity to tell me about these things. But they did not, and they even reported my questioning to my father. He, as usual, responded with anger.

On the other hand life at school was adventurous. To earn some revenue I would easily fall prey to fellow student's schemes. Often I would do their homework to get some money and often their "dinner money" to pay off my part of the tuition fee at school.

One day I got myself into trouble when I copied for three class fellows into their note books my whole essay in the Farsi language class. The teacher quickly recognized the uniformity of handwriting and words and soon I was found out. It was a rule that since it was a language class, we had to speak in Farsi. When I was asked why did I do such a thing, since I did not know much of Farsi I blurted a sentence among many I had memorized. Like a taught parrot I replied, *"Khudai Buzerg wa berter rahnuma'i kardand* – God almighty led me." My teacher looked at me and laughed but then said what I came to know later to mean: "Well, the same God has asked me to cane you for such a lie and plagiarism."

I accepted my lot but was glad that the boys did not take their money back, and I was able to pay my dues to the accounts office at school.

By March 1967, I had passed my final school examinations. However, even before that my father pressed me constantly to make a decision to become an Ahmadi missionary and to begin study in the Ahmadi Missionary College in Rabwah. I knew that apart from financial reasons this would have pleased him and made him more respectable among his friends in the community, but I was determined not to be pushed. Instead, I had in my heart the idea to apply for admission to the other college, the secular college that taught students wanting to go on for careers other than those of the Ahmadiyya Movement. Father was displeased.

"Masood," he asked me one evening, "why are you so set on going to this other college? You know I'm not happy with the idea."

I was about to say, "Father, you never really helped me in my school education, why now are you dictating to me?" but I held on to my peace and answered him, though I am afraid that it was also with some pride in my heart. "Father, I want to make my own way in life. I was born in this home, but it doesn't mean that I must obey the way you follow unquestioningly. It is possible that I might find a better way to live than this. I don't want to have a blind faith. I want to know why it is that when a new branch with new fruit was brought forth out of the Islamic tree it turned into two branches—our own Qadiani party and the Lahore party of the Ahmadiyyas. I want to discover for myself how far the Muslim people are right. And I want to see what the Christian books have to say! Above all I want to be a real Muslim."

My father's face went red, and his neck swelled with anger.

"Masood, stop it!" he roared at me. "I was sorry for my earlier hard words and behavior to you, and I've been tolerant with you up to now. I gave you love of which you are not worthy. I helped you in this so-called research. Harshly I heard what people said about you, but even then I tried my best to provide answers to your eternal questions! I took you to hear our great teachers. Today," and here he smote the cupboard with his hand, "this cupboard holds books that I bought for you but could ill afford. I thought all the time that truth would triumph and you would forget these crazy notions. Even now, I believe you will one day find the light of truth. One day you will repeat with faith the inspired words of *Hazrat Masih-Maood* (Mirza Ghulam Ahmad), 'I will take your message unto the ends of the earth.' I used to think we would have a great name, that our financial problems would be solved, that our days would turn to happiness. But today I see that my hopes in you are vain hopes. You want no part of this dream. You want to live a selfish life and to spoil our reputation. Well, perhaps you've forgotten that I can be a cruel father! If you do not put an end to this nonsense, I will cause you to disappear from the face of the earth."

He paused and looked at me with anger blazing in his eyes.

"Because we are Muslims, I will give you one more chance to accept the truth. Otherwise, prepare yourself for the wrath of God!"

With this he left the room.

I sat wearily on my bed, my mind empty. I looked around my room and saw my books and asked myself, "What has happened to you, Masood? The grief, the hard words; leave these things and flow with the stream. Leave all this behind and do what your father wants.

Live in peace." This happy idea went around in my mind, but another part of me said, "No! This is not the truth, and you know it! Unveil the truth, Masood. Live in the light of it." The words I had written at the end of my Ahmadi doctrine examination paper rose up before me: "I have written, but I do not believe."

Again I thought, "Of what value will it be to you if you prove that the Ahmadi way is wrong? Where will you go then? To conventional Islam? But Islam is also divided. ..."

I was thirsty and depressed. I went through to the kitchen and drank a large glass of water then left the house. Outside the moon was full, and the shadows of the town were comfortable and familiar. The fresh air seemed to sweep away the cobwebs of my mind, and I walked on to the edge of the town, away from the subdued bustle. There I sat down on a big stone and looked at the moon. I felt full of praise for the wise Creator who had made all things so wonderfully. The stars and the moon seemed so perfect and clean when compared with the problems of my world there in Rabwah town.

In my heart I felt a quiet urge to tell God everything. "Take your problems to Him," my heart seemed to say. "He is the great Creator and He can reveal Himself to you. He is the God who can solve your problems. He can do it, for you have a desire to know Him." At this thought, tears came to my eyes. I spread out my hands to the starry heavens and said from a sincere heart, "O God, great Creator, I call upon you to help me. I beg you to lead me to the light and the truth, or else change me so that I will not want to know the truth any more. Why are you silent, O God? I hear about you. I read about you. Now I need to hear you. I need you to lead me." I could say nothing more but just wept, alone in the moonlight.

I found I was near the river again, and as before, it gave me peace and calmness in my heart. Slowly I got to my feet and walked back into the town. And something strange happened. I felt so clearly that I was not alone. Someone was with me on that night walk, and I came back with new strength to continue my search for the truth.

One afternoon a few days later, my father took me to meet the editor of an Ahmadiyya magazine called *Al-Furqan*, The Truth. His name was Mawlana Abul-Atta and he was a respected man in our town. My father greeted him, saying, "I have brought this son of mine to you so that you can advise him. Perhaps he'll listen to you. He needs clear guidance."

My father left us after a little while, and the *mawlawi*, the preacher, said to me, "Masood, your father seems very angry with you. What is the matter?"

Though he asked me sincerely, he continued to be busy with his papers, so I kept silent. He looked up and asked me again, "What are these things that you're saying in the town? Does someone tell you to say all these things? You are just a young boy of seventeen years. It's not usual for someone of your age to have these sort of questions. I think that you are being deceived by the other Muslims. Is it not so? I hear that you are beguiled by the Christians, that you are also studying Christianity. Is this so? Come now, Masood, can you get anything good from ignorant Muslim leaders outside our community? And these 'pastors' and 'reverends' ... they come to these sweepers just to fill their bellies. They don't even know why they call themselves Christians except that their fathers were so-called Christians, and so they are too."

He sat there, waiting for me to reply. I tried to collect my thoughts to answer him, but before I could do so, he said, "Why do you stay silent? Perhaps I'm right when I say that these other people are involved with you in this 'research' and that they are at the root of your dissension." He looked at me shrewdly.

I plucked up my courage and said, "To say that is wrong, *Mawlawi Sahib*. All this research I have done myself from books. I asked the elders for advice and information and you are witness that I have come to you. No one comes to me to talk; I go to them."

I felt quite pleased with that reply, but he interrupted. "What is it you want to know, Masood? What do you really want?"

Boldly I said to him, "To search for the religion that is from the beginning and will continue through all eternity."

"That is Islam, of course," he said shortly.

"But sir, even Islam is divided into sects and groups. Both you and I belong to a group that Islamic scholars say is not Muslim but *kafir*, pagan—infidel. And what will happen if they manage to pass laws against us and treat us as non-Muslims?" I was feeling upset. I was not to know then, of course, that this was going to happen in Pakistan just a few years later.

"Son," he said, not unkindly, "it will not make any difference. We Ahmadi Muslims have the truth for which you are searching. We can help you, but first you must come to us trustfully, believing."

I wanted to say something further, but he turned back to his desk and indicated that the interview was at an end. However, he did say that he would see me again in two days' time. Meanwhile, he gave me a couple of anti-Christian books and a few copies of his magazine, and told me to read them. I spent several days reading them and found that *Mawlawi Sahib* was very good at his points of arguments. Although his ideas were quite convincing, I still wanted to know what really other Muslims and even Christians would respond to his reasoning.

I had kept up occasional visits to the Christian quarter where I had first talked to the Christian preacher, and a few days after my conversation with the *Mawlawi Sahib mawlawi,* I returned there. As I walked down the narrow dirty lane to the sweepers' area, I was eagerly anticipating the meeting. The pastor had also promised to bring me some books. No one saw me turn into the courtyard, and I arrived just as the worship was about to begin. The pastor met me with great kindness, and I sat with the Christians hearing this good man speak of Jesus the Christ known to Muslims as 'Isa al-Masih Ibn Maryam, Jesus the Messiah, the son of Mary' as a loving Saviour and Friend. As always, I was struck by the spirit of the gathering and the love of the pastor. He had few earthly qualifications, but with simple sincerity he preached the word of God. He once said to me, "Son, I do not have much knowledge, but what I do know of the truth I want to share."

After the worship he gave me two books to read. One of them was called *Mirza Ghulam Ahmad Qadiani Exposed*. For a short time we discussed the gospel, then I made my way home quickly.

Back at home I wasted no time but sat down and read both books he had given me. I read them at one sitting, and when I looked up, it was late. I was quite confused. All the suspicions I had begun to have about the founder of our Ahmadi sect seemed to be true, and I did not know what to think.

As agreed, I went within a couple of days to see Mawlana Abul-Atta again in his office, and this time another man, obviously a learned person, was sitting with him. Several other people were there too. After we had greeted each other, I began, "Sir, is it true that Mirza Ghulam Ahmad called himself God and proclaimed that he was greater than Muhammad?"

Hearing this, the *mawlawi* became quite upset and retorted sharply, "What nonsense is this that you're talking?" I was ready for him though, and replied, "But is it not true that in his book *A'ina Kamalat Islam*, he saw in a vision that he was God, and that he believed it? He says that he created heaven and earth!" With some doubt as to how he would receive it, I took out the piece of paper on which I had written out the reference and gave it to him. He took it and read it through.

"On the one side, sir," I said, "Masih-Maood spoke of himself as God it seems, while on the other he clearly states that the person who is born of a woman and who yet calls himself God is worse than an adulterer." (*Noor ul-Quran*, part 2, page 12.)

The two old men looked at each other, and one of them asked me, "Did you read these books for yourself?"

"No," I admitted. "Then how did you come to know of these things? Did someone help you?" Some other boys of my own age were in the office helping to pack bundles of magazines, and they bent forward to listen to my reply. It did not seem good to lie, and I confessed that I had read these things in the book the pastor had given me, *Mirza Ghulam Ahmad Qadiani Exposed*.

"And you believe a book that some Christians or non-Ahmadi Muslims have given you?"

The other old man spoke angrily, "Boy, if you keep on at this you will ruin your life! You will lose your religion and the world besides – *din wa dunya ku do gay.*"

I thanked him for his advice, but said firmly, "Sir, I need answers and *Mawlawi* Sahib promised to give me guidance, and that's why I am here." When I said this, the two gentlemen cooled down a little.

Mawlana Abul-Atta took up the argument. "It is better that you should read these paragraphs that you have given to us in their context. I have some other books for you, but meanwhile, keep in mind that *Hadhrat Sahib* (Mirza Ghulam Ahmad) called himself God by inspiration and revelation in allegorical way. In fact, he was not."

He hesitated to continue the discussion and asked me if I would come some other time. I sensed that he did not want to say too much in the presence of the other boys, in case it undermined their faith, He handed over the books which I took with bad grace, feeling that once again I had received no light, no help and no useful advice. I was becoming vexed with the unwillingness of the elders to face up to the real difficulties I was having. No one was willing to help me find the truth. They only wanted me to believe blindly the things I had been taught from childhood. The *mawlawi* also gave me more books, and I took my leave.

I tried to read the books I had been given by the *mawlawi.* I sensed that all in my family were upset with me, but my father, for once, said nothing. Perhaps he was thinking that at least I was reading books written by Ahmadi writer(s) and that perhaps I would be convinced by them and stop my research. In fact, it was a hopeless exercise, but I persevered and within a few days or so I had finished them. However, I kept on studying them for several months until it was time for me to take my exams. Over my father's objections, I had enrolled in the secular college, and by this time I was approaching the end of my last year there.

After the exams were over, I went one evening to see my friend the pastor who used to come to visit the Christians. He lived in another village and would travel over from time to time to preach the word of God to the Rabwah fellowship and to lead their services. On this evening, as I approached the *bustee*, the colony where they lived in their poor huts, I heard a commotion up ahead. An angry crowd was milling around, and I was told that some of the Ahmadi boys had grabbed the preacher as he came from the bus stand, beaten him in the street and forced him to return to the bus and to his village. The men and women who stood around were very angry with me; they claimed that this had happened because of my interest in Christianity. I was told that I was a disgrace to the Ahmadiyya community.

Earlier that very same day, my father had been called to the *Amoor-i-Ama* office. This is a non-official department that regulates the behavior of the Ahmadis. Though it is a non-government department, it has real power over the social life of the Ahmadi believers, and no one takes it lightly. The interview with my father was brief. "Your son has crossed the boundary," he was told. "He has gone too far in this anti-Ahmadiyya research, and we will bear it no longer. You are to tell him that if he does not cease his activities there will be very serious consequences."

My father was angry. That night he told me spitefully that my "preacher friend" had been barred from entering Rabwah to minister to the sweepers.

"That is not the right thing to do," I protested, but my father laughed mockingly and said, "Our arms are quite long enough to root out and finish off all apostasy."

I felt a sudden stab of fear, but I answered him boldly, "Daddy, even Muslims call us *kafir,* unbelievers. We are the ones who are apostate, they say. We've made our separate mosques, and we don't have fellowship with other Muslims. Is it not strange that we've taken the simple verses of the Qur'an and the Hadith, the traditions handed down to us from the beginning, and we have used them as we wished? The Qur'an teaches us that the Prophet Jesus ascended to heaven, but we have made an explanation to show that really He died in Kashmir and that His tomb can be seen there today. Formerly we believed that Muhammad was the last Prophet, but today we value *Hazrat Masih-Maood* (Mirza Ghulam Ahmad) above Muhammad.

"On the one hand we preach to the Muslims and tell them that Ghulam Ahmad is the *Mahdi,* the great leader expected for hundreds of years, and this way we hope to win them to us. On the other hand we tell the Christians that Mirza Ghulam Ahmad is the Second Coming of Christ. We even say to Hindus that Mirza Ahmad is their Krishna for whom they are waiting. We once had the same ideas of inspiration, revelation, vision and prophecy; all Islam agreed. But now we have our own meanings for these things to help clarify the things that can never be clear!

"Daddy, what does all this mean? I can't understand it, but I want to understand. I must know the truth! I want to be a simple Muslim only. I am fed up with all the nonsense interpretations."

My father's face became as red as a brick, and he came at me out of his chair, intending to throw all the books that were on the table to the ground. Seeing the Qur'an among them he stopped, but instead he dragged me from the chair and began to bang my head hard against the wall, shouting at me as he did so, "You dirty, unclean human being! Today I will not leave you alive! Today I myself will see you into hell!"

Through the pain, I struggled to get away from him, out of the door. I reached the street, but he was too quick for me. Before I could escape, he caught me by the throat and began to squeeze as hard as he could. I tried to cry out, to wriggle out of that suffocating grasp, but his grip was like iron.

I felt my eyes begin to come out of their sockets, and a red light seemed to flash in front of my eyes. I heard my sister, Jamila, crying loudly as I struggled. Apparently some people heard her screams and saw what was going on. They rushed over to help free me from my father's maddened rage. I felt the band around my throat released and tried to speak, but all that would come out was a hoarse gasp. My vocal cords were temporarily injured.

Some people took me to the nearest mosque. There I sat on the veranda, barefoot and shaking with the cold and with shock. A little later the leader of our area, an Ahmadi official, came to me and began to counsel me to make peace with my father and to stop my studies. Others broke in and said that they agreed it must stop. I thought to myself that if this was the price of my studies, then they might not be worth it, but I did not say so. In fact, I could not say anything very much. My throat was very painful, and I could not speak clearly for some time.

Finally I was sent home, but found that my father was unwilling even to have me in the house. He was still furious with me, and only when I asked his forgiveness and finally promised that I would abandon my research, did he reluctantly agree that I could come in. With my lips I agreed to his conditions, but in my heart I felt empty and alone. It was as though someone had abandoned me. It was well into the night before I slept.

Several days later it was the Christian feast of Christmas, December 25, 1968. That day I saw my friend Ahmed again. He was kind and insisted that I go with him to his home. As we walked he joked with me and asked me lightly whether I had received any *eidi* or festival money that day. In Pakistan, we celebrate the birthday of the founder of our state, Muhammad Ali Jinnah, on that day. When we reached Ahmed's home his father was there, but I think that my recent behavior had made him less fond of me, and he made some excuse and left. We were alone in the house then, for Ahmed's mother had gone to Rawalpindi to be with her daughter who had just given birth to a child. Ahmed talked with me and gave me the same advice as others.

"Masood, renounce this stubborn attitude of yours. No good can come of it. You're only making your life miserable."

"I'm not being stubborn, Ahmed. I must have answers. I don't want a cover-up of lies. I want the truth, and I will not be satisfied until I get it. I want the elders to know that they are wrong!"

My pride hurt Ahmed, and he shouted at me for the first time: "Masood, stop this kind of talk. Have you lost all honor for the elders? It's a good thing that you're my friend, or else I'd beat you!

I was immediately full of remorse that I had hurt my friend.

"I'm sorry, Ahmed. Our friendship should not allow us to be rude to each other. Rather, it asks you to help me. Help me in my research, my brother." I pleaded with him, but Ahmed was not agreeable.

"But you've promised your father not to do any research, haven't you?"

I nodded. "That's true," I admitted, "but I was forced to say that. I didn't agree willingly, and I'm not bound by that. Now my research must be underground, and I want you to help me."

Ahmed seemed frightened. He knew what would happen if he was caught helping me.

"I can't help you, Masood. I'm your friend, but the concern of religion is greater than this. I can't allow you to speak a word against it. But anything you do say, you are going to have to prove."

I became upset with his lack of courage. "Give me a pencil and paper!" I demanded. He did so, and I pulled out a list of questions I had with me, and I wrote: Ghulam Ahmad taught that Christ died and that His grave is in Kashmir.

"Now, Ahmed, we Muslims believe that our Prophet cannot make mistakes, but Ghulam Ahmad has made mistakes in connection with this. Look here."

I took up the pencil and wrote again:

1. After escaping death on the cross, Jesus went to Kashmir and lived there for eighty years and died at the age of 120, in Srinagar. But in one of his early books, *Azala-Auham*, Jesus supposedly died in Palestine (page 473).

2. In *Tabligh-Risalet*, volume 8, the age is given as 125 years.

3. In *Tadhkira Al-Shahadatayn* it is recorded that Isa, the son of Mary, lived for 120 years after the crucifixion. Mirza Ghulam Ahmad has written these three things, and they are all different. What are we to believe, that God forgot, or Ghulam Ahmad? And there's something even more interesting, Ahmed. Jesus preached in Jerusalem, Judea and Samaria for only three and a half years and did miracles there. The history books are full of it, and there are many evidences of His life and ministry there, even today. But don't you think it's strange that though He is supposed to have lived in this part of the world for between eighty and 120 years and though He preached here during that time, there is none that believed Him? Research indicates that the grave that is supposed to be His grave in Kashmir is not that of Jesus, but of Prince Yuz Asef! What do you think, Ahmed? Did He not preach after His crucifixion? It's all very strange."

I paused, and Ahmed looked thoughtful as he said to me, "Masood, I will enquire about these things. But I don't have the books here; I must get them from the library."

We talked some more, until his father came home again, then we said goodbye, and I went away. I have always been sorry that Ahmed did not keep his word and get me the books from the library. Days and months passed. I was careful not to cause distress to my parents, my teachers and friends in the community and so kept most of my findings and queries to myself. My days at the Ahmadiyya College were not filled with enthusiasm although I would raise my eyebrow at times at some of the points in lectures of teachers.

_____ 6 _____

Taking a Stand

In September 1969, something took place that forced me to take a stand. Looking back now, I am grateful to God that I did not know what would happen, for had I known it, I may have kept quiet.

It happened after the *Isha* prayer, the late evening prayer of the day, at the mosque in Rabwah. Prayer was over, and there followed a meeting on the subject of the life of Muhammad. Many people stayed for it, and I happened to be there too, sitting on one side. Some of the more mischievous boys of the town also stayed, but I knew that they were only there in obedience after being reprimanded by the elders. From time to time I noticed them looking at me and pointing, and I wondered what they were talking about.

But by this time someone was speaking, and since it was an open meeting, different people came forward, both young and old, and spoke in turn. The last speaker was a former Sunni Muslim, a member of one of the two great branches of Islam, who had become an Ahmadi. He made an impressive figure as he stood there. He was introduced and then began to speak, "Tonight we have seen Muhammad's life from several different angles.

Now I want to see what the Torah, the Law, and the *Injil*, the gospel, have to say about him."

I sat up, very interested. I wondered what this man would say. From my own research, I had come to believe that the *Injil* had nothing to say about Muhammad! Although I was not sure, I believed in the corruption of the Bible by the hands of Jews and Christians.

The man had a Bible with him, and he opened it at Deuteronomy, chapter 18, saying, "God said to Hazrat Mosa (the prophet Moses) that he would raise up a Prophet from among his brethren. It is written here, 'And I will raise them up a Prophet from among their brethren, like unto thee, and will put my words in his mouth; and he shall speak unto them all that I shall command him' (Deuteronomy 18:18). That prophet is Muhammad on whom peace be," he declared boldly "and it is about him that this prophecy was given. Muhammad is the descendant of Ishmael, and Ishmael was the brother of Isaac."

I listened, but not with faith, for it seemed that this was not right. The man continued, "Both Moses and Muhammad were born into idolatrous communities. Both men's relatives ignored and disbelieved them and later came to see that they were truly prophets. Both migrated from their own lands, and both fought against paganism. Both came to the world with the law of God in their hands."

He turned the pages of the Bible to the New Testament.

"*Hazrat Isa* (the Prophet Jesus) has also prophesied about Muhammad."

He opened the gospel of John and turned to chapter 14, verse 16; "And I will pray the Father, and he shall give you another Comforter that he may abide with you forever."

I knew that Christians taught that this referred to the Holy Spirit, but what this man said was a common interpretation among Muslims. He continued, "It is further written in verses 25 and 26 of this chapter, 'These things have I spoken unto you, being yet present with you. But the Comforter, which is the Holy Ghost, whom the Father will send in my name, he shall teach you all things, and bring all things to your remembrance.'

"Then Jesus said in chapter 15, verse 26, 'But when the Comforter is come, whom I will send unto you from the Father, even the Spirit of truth, which proceedeth from the Father, he shall testify of me.'"

Clearly the speaker was trying to show that the Holy Spirit was Muhammad! He continued to quote from chapter 16 of the gospel of John, making his argument stronger, as he thought, and I began to feel very angry with this wrong use of the *Injil*. I remembered the angry exchange with my father when I had challenged him about the dishonest way that the Ahmadis quote Scripture for their own purposes. But still I listened. "I would remind you, my brothers, that these truths are fulfilled in the Prophet Muhammad, peace be upon him. Muhammad is the one who brings all things to remembrance. He brought to remembrance through the Qur'an all the true things concerning Jesus, His life and death, that He was born to the Virgin Mary and that He did miracles. Muhammad has reminded us of the true state of the Christians and the Jews; he has quoted all the important prophets from the time of Adam to his own time. He has guided us into truth indeed and our Prophet has given us a very good law for our lives."

If he had stopped there, that would have been more than enough, but he did not! He began to say that not only were the prophecies about Muhammad true, but that there were also prophecies about Mirza Ghulam Ahmad, the founder of the Ahmadiyya sect. He said very clearly, "The Second Coming of Christ has been fulfilled in Mirza Ghulam Ahmad. He is the Mahdi-Maood, the great leader, the Masih-Maood, the promised Messiah. He is the essence of all the prophets, and he has appeared to us in these last days with the eternal message of peace and security for us all!" Having said this, he sat down.

Listening to this incredible string of fabrications, I felt the blood pound in my veins. "What rubbish!" I said to myself, and in my heart there was a strong gladness, because I *knew* that it was nonsense. I felt that someone was pressing me to speak. "Masood, stand up! It is time to tell what you know to be the truth. Speak it out, or your mind and heart will not be able to stand it!" It was just like a real voice, and dimly, in the background, I heard the leader say, "Is there anyone else who would like to address the assembly?"

He might have been asking me personally! As he spoke these words, I heard a murmur pass through the crowd, and he had the look of a man who feels that perhaps he has said something unwise. But by that time I was on my feet. It was just as though someone— perhaps that same "someone" who spoke to me—put His hands under my elbows and lifted me to my feet. I made my way carefully to the place where the speakers addressed the group. As I passed the man who had just spoken, I asked him if I might borrow the Bible to which he had referred, and he courteously gave it to me.

I felt the eyes of the whole assembly on me. The leader was sitting to one side; I ran my eyes over the group and then began to speak. It was as though another power took hold of my tongue at that moment, and I will never forget the things that were said through me that day.

"*Aziz Sami'ein*—Honorable listeners! Every day we face new experiences and learn new things. And today perhaps you will hear something that's new to you. We have just heard this gentleman speak to us, and he seems to say that he is one who believes the Bible from which he quoted and that it has not changed, though Muslims and Ahmadis say it has been changed."

I stopped and looked down at the Bible I held. I was conscious that I was saying things that would not sound well to the group. I knew that they would be thinking that I, a mere boy of eighteen, had no right to say such things, especially in public. But I continued:

"I must ask the gentleman if it is true as he says that Deuteronomy 18:18 really speaks of Muhammad, how is it that people at the time of Christ pointed to Jesus as the fulfillment of this verse? John 1:45 clearly says that, 'Philip findeth Nathanael, and saith unto him, We have found him, of whom Moses in the law, and the prophets, did write, Jesus of Nazareth, the son of Joseph.' The people of Christ's time said, when they saw His miracles, 'This is of a truth that prophet that should come into the world' (John 6:14). In the Acts of the Apostles, Stephen and Paul pointed to the same prophecy when they spoke of Christ. Jesus spoke of Himself in this way, 'For had ye believed Moses, ye would have believed me: for he wrote of me'" (John 5:46).

It seemed to me as I looked at those listening that all the watching eyes were hostile, but the inner urge to speak was strong.

"Now we come to the supposed similarity between Moses and Muhammad. We have heard some facts, but not others. For example, in Moses' time the King of Egypt killed the Hebrew children, but did this happen in Muhammad's time? No, it did not. Moses spoke to God and was given the title *Kalim ul Allah*, the one who talks to God (Sura 19 verse 52; Sura 4 verse 164). Brethren and my elders, the Qur'an says that Muhammad received his messages from God through the medium of the archangel Gabriel. Further, the prophet Moses did miracles, but the prophet Muhammad did not. I would even say that those who claim that Muhammad did miracles are saying that the Qur'an is lying! For is it not true that the Qur'an makes no mention of any ability of Muhammad to do miracles?

"And now, what of the gospel of John from which it has just been 'shown' that Muhammad is the Holy Spirit promised by Jesus? It is true, is it not, that in our books Mirza Ghulam Ahmad is himself referred to as the Holy Spirit? Right here we have a contradiction. But meanwhile, what does this verse, John 14:16, really mean? Who is this 'other Comforter'?

"Firstly, how can we accept this verse since it clearly refers to God as Father? We are opposed to this doctrine of God as Father, so how can we accept the verse at all?

"Secondly, what is the real significance of this statement of Jesus? Clearly He is so important that when *He* prays to the Father, then the Father will give the Holy Spirit in response. We Muslims say that the Prophet Muhammad is greater than Jesus, but could Muhammad pray this prayer? Jesus spoke clearly when

He said, 'If I go not away, the Comforter will not come unto you; but if I depart, I will send him unto you.' This is found in John 16:7."

I was leafing through the pages of the gospel as I went. I was certain that it was God Himself who was reminding me of these passages!

"Further, in John 14:16 it says that the Holy Spirit will come to 'abide with you forever.' Surely this means just what it says, namely that the Holy Spirit will live eternally with us. Can this really apply to Muhammad? He lived in this desperate and sinful world for sixty-two years! How can anyone think that sixty-two years is eternity?"

Some of the people in the courtyard of the mosque looked at one another. I knew what they were thinking about me. I began to notice the hatred on the faces of some, and others were shuffling their feet restlessly. But I hoped that at least some were thinking about these things, so I continued, "Please notice John 16:13 where it says of the Holy Spirit that 'he shall not speak of himself; but whatsoever he shall hear, that shall he speak.' Perhaps this could speak of Muhammad, for it is true that he spoke that which was given to him from heaven, but what about the next verse? 'He shall glorify me: for he shall receive of mine.'

"Brethren, the Qur'an testifies of the Spirit that he came to Muhammad as Gabriel from God bringing him the message. We Ahmadis believe that the Holy Spirit is Muhammad and that about him Jesus said, 'He shall not speak of himself ... He shall glorify me: for he shall receive of mine.' Now if this is true we must conclude that God is Christ or Christ is God. These words show it clearly. But to us this is surely totally impossible! It is a very bad thought for a Muslim to have! But then, if

Christ is not God, then how is it possible for the Holy Spirit to be Muhammad? If we say that, then we must also believe that the Qur'an was given to Muhammad from Christ and that Christ is God!

"If we still remain unconvinced, then what do we make of the Holy Spirit who is spoken of in the *Acts of the Apostles* in the Bible? A disciple of Jesus, the one called Peter, denied even knowing him, three times, but when the power of the Holy Spirit descended on this man, he spoke with great courage and boldness to a multitude of people when he said, 'Ye men of Israel, hear these words; Jesus of Nazareth, a man approved of God among you by miracles and wonders and signs, which God did by him in the midst of you … Him … ye have taken, and by wicked hands have crucified and slain… let all the house of Israel know assuredly, that God hath made that same Jesus, whom ye have crucified, both Lord and Christ'" (Acts 2:22-23, 36).

I was amazed at the boldness with which I read these fiery words. As I held the book from which I had read them, I was acutely aware of the power of God present in the mosque that evening. I held my breath for a moment. What other strong words would follow? I felt I must say one final thing: "Having heard these things, brethren, why do we listen to wrong teaching and to debates in which there is no truth?"

If I had stopped there I believe that would have been best, but I would not be silent. I felt that I was a great person, and in my heart I was proud that God was with me. Being young and foolish and inflated with this pride, I continued to speak, rashly attacking the idea that Ghulam Ahmad was the Messiah or Christ.

"What is the truth we are to believe? I hear it said that our founder, Mirza Ghulam Ahmad, has come in the form of Christ. If this is so, then sirs, I dare to ask what happened to those signs that are mentioned in the Bible and stated in the traditions of Islam? Christ's disciples foretold that when Jesus comes the heavens shall pass away with a great noise and the elements shall melt with a fervent heat. Elsewhere it is written that a disciple said, 'Behold, he cometh with clouds; and every eye shall see him.'

"Obviously there are very few people in the world that know of Mirza Ghulam Ahmad. According to us Ahmadis he was to challenge and convert all Christians to Islam before he died. But has it happened? I ask again, what *is* the truth we are to believe ...?"

A tremor passed through me. In my heart I felt a shiver of fear and a voice inside me said, "Masood, stop it! Sit down!"

My legs trembled, and I tried again to speak. Dimly I saw the crowd surge, and my father came towards me. With his hand he struck me a mighty blow, and I fell to the floor. Above me people pushed to strike at me, to kick me. Mercifully, the darkness closed in, and I slipped into unconsciousness.

7

Flight!

I came to my senses on a bed in the local hospital. Looking around dizzily, I saw other patients in bed and knew I must be in the general ward. I tried to push myself up, but I could not move. Outside I could hear the traffic on the main road. I was feeling as weak as a newborn baby.

A nurse came in carrying a hypodermic syringe. She said nothing, just gave me an injection, and after a few moments it seemed that I was floating in the air! Then I must have slept, for the next time I opened my eyes my friend Ahmed was standing by the bed looking down at me, unsmiling. He had two other young men with him. I tried to smile at Ahmed, but I did not succeed very well, for I still felt ill and dizzy. One of the young men laughed loudly and said mockingly, "Next time he had better not be so courageous, now that he sees where his hastiness has brought him!"

The other one nodded and said, "He's a great man, all right. Two days since his 'accident' and he's still alive, though bedridden." By this I knew that it must be the third day since I had been admitted.

Ahmed gestured for them to leave so that we could talk. They finally went, and he sat on the chair beside my bed and said to me earnestly, "Masood, why are you darkening your future like this? Not only you will be affected by this nonsense of yours, but your family too. Think of them, Masood. There's still time to put an end to this. Why don't you confess that you've been wrong and hasty and that you're willing to make things right in Rabwah. Accept the right way, brother, and everything will be well for you." Hearing his words, and seeing his love for me, I felt sad. He helped me to sit up in the bed, and my eyes filled with tears as I said, "Ahmed, are you too treating me as a liar? Why have you of all people become my enemy? I can't understand what I do! I feel that someone has told me to say these things, Ahmed. I feel it inside me, and I must speak." Ahmed frowned seemingly, "Masood, you *are* a liar. That someone has flesh and blood, and you know it! Someone has taught you to say these things against us, haven't they?"

Despite his words, I knew that he had my best interests at heart. He looked worried, not believing my words. I tried again to explain.

"Ahmed, when I spoke there at the mosque, obedient to this voice inside me, everyone listened. They were completely silent. You know that. But as soon as I added my own words and spoke as I did just before they beat me, I lost! I lost the calm in my heart, my peace of mind — and they beat me, Ahmed."

I looked up at him hopefully. I wanted him to understand me, but he just answered me angrily, as he jumped up, "Now I really believe that you're mad. The doctor's right. You should go to a mental hospital."

And he turned away without saying goodbye to me and went out in anger.

It saddened me that he went like that, but even more, I was alarmed at his reference to the doctor. Was the doctor treating me as though I was mad? It was very unpleasant, and I had the uneasy feeling that something was about to happen. I plucked at the sheet fearfully, weeping silently, wondering what would become of me, too agitated even to pray.

In a few minutes a nurse came to take my pulse. Turning her head to the door, so that no one could come in unawares, she said slowly and clearly, "Beware! Don't eat any food they bring you. Tonight at three o'clock go to the toilet. You'll find your clothes there. Put them on and run. Don't stay here."

She left. I was breathless and forgot instantly all that Ahmed had said to wound me. What had she said? What would happen to me? It was then that I prayed for God's help and lay there anxiously. How slowly the hours passed that day.

Who was this girl? Just an ordinary nurse? I thought much about her strange warning as I lay on my bed, and I realized that she surely spoke the truth. The thought made me breathless for a moment. How could she know? It must be God who had sent her. He had sent his "angel" to warn me!

That evening food was brought to me. I looked at it suspiciously. I was hungry, but the warning was ringing in my ears: "Don't eat any food they bring you." I looked at it again. Would they really try to poison me? I knew that it was not unknown for apostate people to be killed in one way or another. Was it really true that I had denied my heritage? I did not know clearly what I believed. Furtively, I scraped the food into a plastic bag, put it into a drawer and prayed. I prayed to God again and again to protect me. I recited many suras of the Qur'an from memory. Every minute seemed like an hour, and when anyone came to the door to look at me, I pretended to be asleep.

The night seemed endless. There was a small nightlight in the ward, so the nurses on night duty could check on us all in the same room. At about 3 a.m., the door was opened quietly, and someone called me, softly. I slipped out of bed, my heart beating loudly, and tiptoed through the door to the toilet. I went inside and found my own clothes, the shirt and trousers that I had been wearing when I had been assailed, and I put them on.

When I came out my "angel" was waiting, and she said urgently, "If you go to the other side of the garden you'll be able to climb up on the wall and jump over. You won't be hurt. At about 4.30, a bus will pass, and it will take you to Lyallpur. From there, take another bus to Lahore. The address where you can go and be safe is in your pocket. I have put some money there, too. My mother lives there, and she'll help you. I've written her a letter explaining all this. Give it to her as soon as you arrive."

I was amazed and confused by all this. It seemed like something out of one of my boys' adventure stories! Why was this girl helping me, I wondered. Why should she care about me? More than ever I was sure that God had sent her at just the right time, and I thanked her with faltering words.

But she was pushing me outside. I asked her, "Why are you doing this?"

She said quickly, "This is not the time for questions! You're in danger. This morning a high official came, and I heard him and your father tell the doctor that you should be killed."

Her eyes were bright with tears, and she said something strange, "This way you, my brother, will live. May
God care for you!"

She disappeared almost before I had time to thank
her. I crept down the corridor and fortunately no one
heard me. Then I was outside in the garden and made
my way cautiously across the lawn. The hospital security man was sitting on a stool near the gate half asleep,
but the bushes hid me from his sight. It was a joke with
us that security men were usually securely asleep, and
this time I was glad that he did not hear me. I could
make out the dark shape of the low wall behind some
more bushes ahead, and I quickly skirted them and
stumbled into a pile of dung! It smelt awful, but I did not
delay. I glanced up, but the security man was still asleep,
and I climbed up onto the wall. I looked down, afraid for
a moment to jump, but at that moment a dog barked,
and I jumped, afraid that I might be seen on the wall. I
landed heavily in some rubbish at the foot of the wall, in
the dusty road. Some pieces of glass cut my hands, but it
seemed that I had landed on a large carton which at
least spared my clothes from becoming more dirty than
they were already. I jumped up and ran to the nearest
big shadow to hide, but no one called out, and I was safe.

After a few minutes, I got to my feet and began to
walk towards Chiniot, five miles away, along the main
road.

There was no moon to light my way as I walked. I
could make out the figures of other Punjabi security
guards, dressed in their *salwar kamiz* "uniform." Most
of them carried lathes, a sort of night stick, with which
they could beat intruders, but few even seem to need to
use them! Most of them seemed to be sleeping, and all
was quiet as my footsteps fell softly in the dust of the

road. The rocky hills around Rabwah were shrouded in darkness and I wondered forlornly, if I would ever be able to come back here safely. The night was cool after the heat of the day, and at any other time I might have enjoyed the evening walk—but not tonight.

I was afraid. I was sure that if I was caught escaping like this I would surely be killed. Thinking about this, I broke into a run, anxious to leave Rabwah behind me, and I ran until I was exhausted. My stay in hospital had made me a little weak, and I was sorry then that I had not taken the bus. But as I had thought more about the nurse's plan, I had not been sure that the bus would be safe, and so had decided to make for Chiniot, where I knew I could catch a train to Lahore in the morning. Again the "someone" in my heart, seemed to urge me to do this, and I felt peace growing in my mind even as I hurried along the side of the dusty road.

In the early morning, an hour or so later, I reached the railway station. Over the door of the station the name "Chiniot" welcomed me. Already the small building was a buzz of activity. People were drinking hot sweet tea. They say that in Pakistan the railway stations never sleep, and this is true. I got into a long queue and eventually bought a ticket for the seven-hour trip to Lahore; then I boarded the waiting train. In a few minutes the diesel engine gave a long whistle, and we moved slowly off in the direction of Lahore.

The train was very full, and even the aisles were crowded. I did not mind, though, for among the crowds I seemed to be safer, more anonymous. After a station or two the crush eased, and I was able to find a seat. People got out to stretch their legs and to buy some food for their breakfast. Some coolies, or porters, pushed through with loud cries as they carried heavy head-loads of bedding rolls and baskets. Because of my excitement I was not hungry, though I had not eaten for many hours, but I did buy some tea. The scalding liquid, sweet as honey, tasted very good on that cold morning. The excitement of the previous night seemed far away, and I was feeling depressed and alone. But I was not alone. ...

I reached in my pocket for the letter the nurse had given me. I turned it over slowly and read the address: Nisbet Road, Lahore. The envelope was not stuck down, and being very curious to see what she had said about me, I opened it and read it. She had told her mother that I had a number of problems that made it necessary for me to leave Rabwah for a while. She asked her mother to take care of me and send me to one of her uncles, so that I should be looked after. She said that she would write again and commended me to her mother's care.

I folded the letter carefully and put it back in the envelope. I felt quite light hearted after reading it, sure that God was looking after me. Outside the train the countryside, green after the rains, looked like heaven to me, and I waited eagerly to get to Lahore.

Some hours later we reached the main railway station of Lahore. I moved slowly out of the long low building, carried along by the crowd, and hired a *tanga*, a horse cart, a common form of transport in our country. The driver asked me where I wanted to go. I reached into my pocket to check the address, and my heart went cold. The envelope and the money the girl had given me were gone! Someone had picked my pocket, probably in the crowd at the station. I felt angry with myself for being so careless, but there was nothing I could do.

I told the *tangawala*, the driver, that my money had been stolen. Surprisingly, he was very sympathetic and offered to take me to Nisbet Road. Fortunately, I had remembered part of the address, so I was able to tell him that much. No other passengers appeared who might have shared the ride with me and thus given him some fare for his trouble, so he flicked the reins over the back of his horse and we left.

He took me right to Nisbet Road and dropped me there. I was very thankful for his kindness. Once more, it seemed that I was being cared for, and I whispered a short prayer of thanks.

I felt shy about asking the whereabouts of the woman's home. This was not done in Pakistan. Had it been a man, I could have asked the shopkeepers along the road. Nevertheless, I could think of no other way to find this woman's house, so I forced myself to ask for her.

No one seemed to know her at all. I stood in the road, wondering what to do. Then, wandering along a little further I came to a large crossroads, known as *Laxmi Chowk*. The whole area was a mass of film hoardings, advertising all kinds of films. Pakistan and India are two of the greatest users of films in the world, and this area was the centre of the film industry in Lahore. The city was famous for its studios, and many young people run away from home and go there secretly, hoping to be able to act in the films. There seemed to be cinemas everywhere and more restaurants than I had ever seen in my life! The crush of traffic was stifling me, and I stepped off the pavement, crowded with people rushing in all directions, and was almost knocked down by a car. I jumped back onto the footpath, straight into a boy. He was carrying a tray holding a teapot and some cups. When I bumped into him, he stumbled and dropped the tray; the china was smashed!

I felt terrible. The boy began to abuse me in angry Punjabi and demanded five rupees for the broken china. I felt completely helpless for I had no money. As usual whenever there is an accident people gathered around quickly. I could see that some of them were wondering if there would be a fight, but I had no desire to argue. I was wrong and very ashamed. I said, "I have no money at all. You can search me if you want, but you won't find one paisa, not the smallest coin."

One old man behind me muttered, "They all say the same thing, these rootless young people who come to the city hoping to find work in the films, hoping to be actors. I suppose he's just the same."

My ears burned. Little did he know the truth, but I had no mind to try to convince him that I had run away because my life was in danger. I spoke to the boy instead, "Look, I'm sorry about the teacups. Why don't I come with you to the restaurant where you work, and I can work too. That way I can earn the money to pay you for the broken things."

The boy was silent for a minute, but then he nodded. I think he was relieved that he would not have to pay for the breakages himself.

"Come on," he said, and I went with him.

He told me that his name was Farukh. He seemed a kind boy, and I felt that he would be a good friend. He was about my own age. He took me to the owner of the restaurant who was sitting at his table at the door counting money. It was a small place, like so many around there, selling mostly tea, both on the premises and outside. Boys like Farukh were everywhere, carrying trays of teacups to different businesses and offices. Everyone drank tea, all the time, and it was a good business. The boys might get some small salary, but they would make more by charging a little extra for the tea they took to customers outside. They were usually not unhappy, but it was hard work and the hours were long.

The man looked up from his piles of cash and stared at me as Farukh recounted the story of the accident. When he had finished, the man said harshly, "So you too, eh? You've run away from home because you have fallen in love with a *filmi* heroine! Which one do you fancy?"

I was embarrassed, for nothing was further from my mind. I kept silent, and he said roughly, "Take him to wash the pots with the other boys."

He dismissed me with a gesture of his hand. Farukh took me to the kitchen, and I began to help with the washing of the piles of utensils. I had been used to helping in this task for years, since I was a small child, but today ... today I felt tears pricking at my eyes, and I impatiently wiped them away with my hand. But not before Farukh had seen me do it.

Late that evening when it was almost time for the restaurant to close, I began to think about where I could stay that night. It seemed hopeless to try to look for the woman in Nisbet Road any further, and I wondered dully whether the nurse back in Rabwah would think that I had simply not bothered to go to her, or that I did not appreciate her kindness. The thought made me sad. As I trudged out into the night, Farukh came up beside me.

"Do you have any place to stay tonight?"

I shook my head, feeling very sorry for myself.

"Follow me then," he ordered, and set off briskly towards the park. He had a natural authority, and I wondered again what his background was, where he had come from. I went after him.

We entered the park, the famous Lawrence Gardens, and sat down on a bench. He told me, to my surprise, that this was his bench. He hired it to sleep on!

"Tonight," he said magnanimously, "we will share it. You can have half and I will have half!"

I was very pleased by his generous thought and thanked him warmly. I watched while he opened a paper bag and took out some small items of food that he laid out carefully on the bench. The way he set the food told me quite a lot about him, and he later confirmed that he had come from a wealthy family from the southern city of Karachi. Karachi, the biggest city in Pakistan, some 800 miles southwest of Lahore, seemed as far away as the moon!

Farukh was a gentleman! The scanty meal we shared that night under the stars did much to fill my stomach and even more the empty void in my heart that I had felt since I had left Rabwah. Once more, I felt that God knew all about me. Certainly, I thought, He had provided my new friend so that I would be cared for that night. Farukh told me his story briefly. A son in an affluent family, he had come to Lahore without his parents' permission to try to get a place in the film world there. It had not worked out, as indeed it had not for so many like him, and he was left penniless. He seemed very unhappy as he told me his story, and I am sure it was very hard for him to have to wash dishes and serve tea. He did not know what the future held for him any more than I did. As I had that morning, he wept a little as he spoke.

We talked late into the night about many things. Farukh, who had been so cross with me that morning, became my true friend. I thought a lot as he spoke. and as so many times before, I became angry at the blind belief that kept us young people in hell! Our elders only wanted to keep their traditions; they had no desire to know the truth. They were not open to God or men! And all of us were bound by this system of thinking and acting. Why, I thought savagely, did people marry and have children just to make them miserable! Life was very difficult for young people. When I spoke of these things to Farukh he was in agreement for the most part, but he insisted that he did not want to live without the love of his parents. I asked him why he did not go back to Karachi. After a moment, he said, "If I went back, would you come with me?"

I was touched by his offer, but all I could think of to say was, "I have never been to Karachi. Where could I live?"

Farukh insisted that this wasn't a problem, and at last I agreed that if he decided to return to Karachi, then I would go with him.

I don't know when we finally slept, though it must have been the early hours of the new day. We slept huddled on the bench, curled up together, sharing the small space. Sometime during the night, the security man came with his *lathi,* his stick, and woke us. Farukh gave him a fifty-paisa coin, and when the guard pointed at me with his stick, he gave him another. The man pocketed the coins and walked on to the next bench where he went through the same procedure with another man. I understood then that this payment was baksheesh, a bribe to allow us to sleep on the bench! This sort of thing is quite common where wages are low. It is the only way people can supplement their incomes. Gratefully I slipped back into sleep....

Around me the houses crumbled to dust with a great roar. Big buildings collapsed into rubble and the earth heaved and shook. Destruction was everywhere. From the gutters and drains an evil smell arose, and the streets were emptied of every living thing. Carrion birds, vultures and kites, wheeled ceaselessly across the sky.

In different places I saw empty mosques, and under the broken wall of the nearest mosque the imam was half buried. I stooped and pulled him out. He did not speak, or even acknowledge my presence, but simply walked away as though in a trance.

As I watched him, I became aware of hundreds of people moving slowly in the same direction. I joined them to see what they were going to do. Ahead of us I saw a great fire, the greatest I had ever seen. Thick clouds of smoke rose into the sky, and the fire was so extensive that I could not see how far it reached. It seemed that the whole world was on fire! People came right up to the fire, and in scores, silently, they stumbled into the heart and heat of it. There was no end to them. It seemed that they were drawn into the flames by a power over which they had no control. As they entered the fire they burned like plastic and became as black as ash.

Seeing this, I was petrified with fear. I shouted at one of the passing men, "Stop this. Stop it! Why are you committing suicide like this?' But he gently freed himself from my grasp and said, "Don't you know that this is the judgment of the world? We are receiving our just reward for what we have done while we were in the world. Horrified, I cried out, "No! I cannot have an end like this. No!" I heard the man say to me, "What are you doing here? Travel to the south. Travel to the south!"

I fled from the great fire, sobbing for breath. I ran until I could run no more and fell to the ground. The place where I fell was like a most beautiful garden but not such a garden as can be compared to those of this world. The atmosphere was calm and tranquil, and ahead of me I saw a great white stone. On it was written these words, "Those are here who have the seal on their foreheads."

I awoke from this awful dream to the loud ringing *adhan* from the Sunni mosque nearby, and for a few moments listened to the familiar words with pleasure:

Ashhado un La Ilaha illallah
Muhammadar-Rasulullah

Farukh stirred in his sleep, and I awoke fully. I got up and went to the mosque from which the call to prayer had come. As I washed my face in preparation for prayer, the thought came to me, "This is not right. Ahmadis do not pray with Sunnis or Shi'ites." However, I put the thought out of my mind and went into prayer. During the prayer time, the imam, the prayer leader, recited the verses from the Qur'an.

"Praise be to Allah, Lord of the worlds, the Beneficent, the Merciful, Owner of the Day of judgment. Thee alone we worship; Thee alone we ask for help. Show us the straight path, the path of those whom Thou hast favoured, not the path of those who earn Thine anger, nor of those who have gone astray."

A strange thought broke in on my prayer. I asked myself, "All us Muslims repeat these words many times in the five daily prayer times. We are all always asking God to show us the straight path. Show us what straight path? Are we not already on the straight path? Has He not already shown us that path? Surely we are always on that path." My thoughts went round and round, but I rebuked myself and squeezed my eyes shut to concentrate on the prayer.

After prayer, the crowd emerged from the mosque and began to disperse. All of a sudden the earth began to heave and shake as it had done in my dream! It was an earthquake, and people were crying out in the streets, "Oh, God, have mercy on us. Have mercy!"

The blood seemed to stop flowing in my veins as I remembered my dream. For a few more moments the earth shook, but then it stopped, the dust settled, and everything was peaceful once more. But my legs trembled still as I saw in my mind's eye the procession of drugged people walking to judgment. My dream was all too clear!

I hurried back to Farukh and found him wide awake as I expected. He had never experienced an earthquake before. We went back to the restaurant and had some breakfast, after which the owner agreed to let me work again for the day. All the boys were on daily rates, and this way they were able to eat at least. And in each of their hearts was the earnest hope and desire that they might one day meet the person who would be able to introduce them to the film world that they craved.

I worked hard, but my mind was not on my work. Again and again, my thoughts went back to my reflections in the mosque. I felt that I had been cheated. "Masood," I said to myself, "tell me, how many times do you pray each day, and how many times do you repeat the same verses from the Qur'an in your prayer like a trained parrot? Did you ever think about what you were supposed to be praying? What does it mean to you when you pray to God, 'Show us the straight path?' If all Muslims believe that they are on the right path, the very path of God's favour, why then do they pray this way, as if they were not, as if they feared that they might miss it?" I realized numbly that I was just as they were. We were all in the same position. Did I really know I was on the straight path? Did my conscience tell me that I was pleasing God? At the end of the day, as I threw out the last of the dirty water, my heart was still crying out to him, "O God, lead me in the way that leads to the truth!"

_____ 8 _____

To the South

Three days went by, and still I had no clear idea what I should do. I continued to work at the restaurant with Farukh, and more and more I came to appreciate his helpful spirit. The owner obviously liked him and trusted him with a number of different jobs.

At the end of the fourth day, after work, I dried my hands and went to find Farukh. We said goodnight to the others and walked outside into the cool air of the night. Suddenly, Farukh said to me, "Come on, Masood. We're going to the railway station."

I was surprised and hurried to catch up with my friend, who was walking quickly in that direction. I caught him by the arm and said, "What did you say? How can we go anywhere, brother? We have no money." Farukh did not turn around but kept walking quickly. "It's OK, Masood. I was given my salary today, and I have a hundred rupees!"

Without waiting for my reply, he hailed a tanga, and we both climbed up into the frail-looking vehicle. I felt confused by his words for, as far as I knew, Farukh could not be getting a salary of anything like that much. I wondered what it was he had done for the owner that he should be paid such a large sum. But there was no time to ask him, for soon we were at the station.

We got down from the tanga and Farukh paid the tangawala a few paise for the ride. He marched up to the enquiry counter, which was besieged with crowds of people all wanting information at once about trains, and eventually came back triumphantly. He announced that there was a train to Karachi in half an hour, and then he went and bought the tickets. We sat together in the passengers' waiting hall, a large open space where those holding the cheapest, third-class tickets waited with their huge bundles of bedding, cheap suitcases and pots and pans. As we sat there, I wondered why it was that people in Pakistan felt obliged to carry all their belongings when they went by train! The contrast with our own pitiful possessions made me depressed. Neither of us had even a bedding roll.

I started to say something about this to Farukh, but I noticed my friend was looking worried, so I said instead, "What's the matter, Farukh? Why are you so concerned?" He looked away and said nothing. I did not want to press him, so we sat in silence. Eventually, with a great noise and a squeal of brakes, the long train came into the station, and we pushed our way into the unreserved compartment with hundreds of others all trying to do the same.

It was not until we had passed about three stations that Farukh finally told me what was bothering him. Keeping his voice low so that no one would hear him, he said to me, "The hundred rupees were not mine, Masood. The owner gave me the money to buy tea for the shop, and the thought just came to me that this was the time to go to Karachi."

I could not find it in my heart to reproach him, though I felt worried about what he had done. The train sped on into the night, and the coaches rocked with their heavy loads.

All through the night and the next day, the train moved slowly through country that I had never seen before. Sometime after Multan, very early in the morning, we crossed the great Sutlej River, and I marveled at the size of the bridge. Now we were in a dry desert-like region, and it was very hot in the train. However, it all seemed new to me after my simple life at Rabwah all these years, and I was filled with excitement. Farukh was infected by my enthusiasm and forgot his own troubles to explain a number of things to me about the countryside. He was on his way home, and every hour that passed brought him nearer to it, though he could not be sure of the welcome he would receive from his family.

In the afternoon the train stopped for some time, and we got down with many others to see what had happened. There had been an accident, it seemed. A man had tried to cross the tracks on his bicycle in front of the speeding train, and he had been killed. His bicycle lay, a twisted heap of metal, to one side of the tracks while various officials rushed around. It was some time before we left the place, and as the train slid past the remains of the bicycle, I thought sadly of the cheapness of human life in Pakistan. Surely a man had a right to die with dignity, even if he could not live with dignity! But now the train was gathering speed, and my thoughts were left behind.

Towards evening, the train stopped at a station, and we bought food packets of rice and fish. The fish was bad, but we forced ourselves to eat it all. Farukh became silent again, not wanting to talk. We crossed the massive Indus River by another long bridge at Hyderabad, and within a few more hours we were at Karachi. The train was very late, and the long journey had made us tired and stiff, but once we came out from the bustling station all our tiredness fell away. Farukh led me out into the main road near the railway station then turned to me and said, "It's good to be home again. I wonder what my parents will think?"

Together we reached the bus stop, and shortly after we were able to squeeze onto a bus that would take us to the home of Farukh's parents. I was weary, and the packed bus was very uncomfortable. I suggested to Farukh that we should wait for the next bus, but he would not hear of it.

"No, we'll stay on this one, Masood. There aren't that many buses, and the next will be just as full as this one. Better we go now."

I resigned myself to the crowded bus. While we waited for it to set off, I wondered what Farukh's parents would think about me. What would I tell them about myself? I had said very little to Farukh about the reasons for my being in Lahore when we met, and he had not been too inquisitive. I allowed him to think that I had run away just as he had. But, I wondered, would his parents accept that story? Would they want to get in touch with my family in Rabwah? Would they be content to have an Ahmadi living in their home even for a brief time? I did not know the answers to these questions and decided that I should wait until such problems were raised, if at all. However, I did hope fervently that they would not think that it was I who had led Farukh astray!

The bus rattled across rough roads for about half an hour before Farukh called to me to hurry as the bus was drawing up at our stop. What happened next was so strange that, looking back, I can only feel that it was God Himself who arranged it all.

Just as Farukh was jumping off the bus, it suddenly speeded up. This is the way that bus drivers often do things in Pakistan. They have heavy schedules, and their buses are overloaded all the time. If they stop completely, it takes too much time to get the bus going again, so they often do not quite stop, and people have to scramble on and off as best they can. Since there were only a couple of us getting off and no one waiting at the bus stop, the driver probably considered this perfunctory slowing down to be quite sufficient.

I saw with horror that Farukh had jumped, but with the bus accelerating I could not jump without great risk of injury on the dark road outside. I cried out to the conductor to stop and let me off, but he retorted angrily, "Were you sleeping, donkey? Can't you get off a bus?"

I was upset, and replied, "That was my friend who got off just now. I'm new here and don't know the way. How shall I meet up with him again?"

The conductor put out his hand, palm upward and shrugged, "You can get off at the next stop and walk back, or perhaps he'll come there and meet you."

He moved off down the bus, clicking his ticket punch to remind the passengers to pay their fares.

The next stop was about a mile further on, and this time I was ready. I jumped off the bus as it approached the stop and for a moment I stood there, watching the friendly red tail lights of the bus receding behind a cloud of dust. The sound of the engine faded, and I was there alone in the street, without a friend, not knowing where to go. At that moment a man passed, and I stopped him and asked him where the last stop was. He told me, and I marched off quickly in that direction, hoping that Farukh would have the sense to wait for me. I would have liked to have taken another bus back, but I had no money in my pocket, and thinking of the distance, I began to run.

Farukh had gone! There in the dark I wept against a wall. On the road a stream of cars rushed past in the humid night, and many people waited for buses that would take them to their homes, to families and food. I had nothing to look forward to in this strange city, now that Farukh had disappeared, and I felt close to despair. It was the last week of September 1969, and I was eighteen years old. I think that was the lowest point in my life.

My immediate problem was finding a place to spend the night. It was getting late, and I had no money. If I went to the mosque, it was possible that the imam, or someone else, might ask me for my story and then he might call the police. They would certainly return me to my parents, and my plight would be worse than before. Likewise, if I slept in one of the parks I would probably be asked for a bribe that I could not pay, and again I might find myself sent back to my parents. The security man would probably hand me over to the police if he was not sufficiently bribed.

It was the hour of *Isha*, the evening prayer, and almost by force of habit, I went to the mosque. After it was over I went outside and followed the main road, not knowing where I was going. After a couple of hundred yards the road ended abruptly, and in front of me there was a dry stream bed. Alongside the stream bed lay a number of huge cement pipes, and the thought immediately came to me that they were big enough to sleep in. In fact, it is not uncommon for poor people to live in these pipes, often for months or even years, before they are used in water projects. It seemed an ideal spot for me, and as I was tired out the pipe I entered far from the road seemed like a soft bed to me. I was a little afraid of snakes and scorpions, particularly since this was the time of warm wet weather, and they seek out cool places at this time of year. But I had no choice. I had to have a place to sleep, and it seemed that God had provided this place especially for me.

I sat in my pipe, watching the road far in the distance. I heard the faint noise of the traffic, and I thought again of the incidents of the past days. A feeling of hopelessness came over me. Everyone who had helped me, I had lost. First, the kind nurse had given me a letter with an address that would provide shelter for me, and I had lost it. Then, coming to this strange city, I had lost the only friend I had. It seemed I was quite alone. But then again the thought came to me that somehow God knew. And I feared — would He, even now, somehow lose me?

I cried out to Him, "O God, are you playing with me? What's all this about? Why am I alive? Can't you tell me what you want me to do? Show me what you plan for my life. I'm not asking you to speak to me in the same way as you spoke to the prophets. I know I'm not a prophet, but I am a creature of your creation. People call me headstrong, agnostic, pagan, apostate! Lead me, O God, as in the past you led those you loved. I want to be your friend. I have no friend, not a single one. I want to speak with you and tell you what has happened to me. Look at me, O God. I have traveled hundreds of miles in my quest. I know you're near to me, as near as the arteries in my body. Talk to me!"

I ended my prayer with a kind of sob.

The next moment, I sat up. A voice was speaking to me, and the voice was kind and mellow: "You are right! I am living in each part of your mind and heart."

My heart leapt. I looked around quickly, but as I thought, it was not the voice of a man that I heard. I felt carried away with joy, and peace flooded through me. I felt as if I was flying, high in the sky. God cared! He talked to me! He did know! He loved me!

I came back to earth again. There seemed to be the awareness of a Presence that had been there with me, and had just left. Strange thoughts took hold of me. Who was it that had been here with me? I looked around again. The darkness and the trees hemmed in the place where I was sitting, and the thought came to me that I was near the edge of the jungle. There were strange superstitions in this region. ... But could it have been God? What nonsensical thought is this? Could God, the Holy, unapproachable God come to this dirty unholy place to a scruffy youth dressed in grimy sweat-soaked clothes? The very thought made me uneasy, but that voice ...! The voice had said, "I am living in you. ...

It was too much. I scrambled to the end of my pipe and stood up, but it was raining, and I could not leave even if I wanted to. I did not want to catch cold. As I stood there wondering, I felt something wet and cold brush against my leg. I jumped back in fright, but it was only a dog. I lay down in the pipe, but I do not know what time sleep came. I awoke in the grey dawn, and the stream bed was quite full of water, and a little water was coming in at the end of the pipe. The dog had gone, and the earth had turned to mud. Leaving the pipe, I walked back to the road and then to the mosque for morning prayer.

I did not know what to do with myself, so I just began to walk, aimlessly. I was so hungry I could have cheerfully eaten the scraps of food that were left on the plates of those eating in the restaurants along the roads. Seeing them, I thought of Farukh and of our time in Lahore together working in the restaurant. I wondered how he was and whether his parents had been glad to see him come home again. What of my own parents? Would they welcome me if I went home? I put the thought out of my mind, for I had no money to go home even if I had wanted to. I kept walking.

My wanderings brought me to the spacious cantonment area. This part of the city has many trees and some open spaces. It used to be the military area when the British ruled our country. On one side of the road there was a big park, Jahangir Park, and opposite it I saw a signboard with the words, "Church of Scotland" on it. On both sides of the road the buyers and sellers of old cars haggled noisily. I crossed the road and entered the compound around the church. I could see no one in the church. It was closed. In the corner of the compound a man was sitting on a *charpai,* and some children were playing nearby. They stopped and watched me silently as I approached the man. He spoke to me, without greeting me, "Where are you going?"

I told him that I would like to see the priest of the church. He said rather roughly that he was not there and that I should come some other day if I wanted to meet him. I heard one of the children say, "He's a Muslim!" Another disagreed, saying, "He's a CID [special police] man!" The man waved to them to be quiet.

"This is private property. You must not come here without permission. We don't know who you are. You don't even seem to know the name of the priest you want to see."

As he spoke a woman, perhaps his wife, came up to us and began to abuse me. "Who are you? I think you're a spy or a *goonda*, [ruffian]. Aren't you the person who was insulting my daughter the other day, along with those other *goondas*? Why have you come here? You must get out."

She said many other unkind things, and I tried to stop her by saying, "*Bibi* [Madam], I don't know what you are talking about. I've come all the way from Punjab to meet any pastor who is able to help me in my quest." But she refused to listen. Seeing her so adamant, the man also insisted, and I had to leave.

I went back to the park I had seen over the road and found a seat there. After a little while, I decided to investigate the reading room I noticed there and went inside to look at the daily newspapers. It seemed to me that on every page was the word "hunger," so I left! Somehow the day passed while I idly watched the flow of people and tried to forget how hungry I was.

It was now getting on towards evening, and the gnawing hunger in my stomach had subsided to a dull ache. I knew that I had to eat something today, but I did not know how I could get food. I was too ashamed to beg for it. Then on a bench near mine two men got up leaving behind them an envelope; a large brown envelope with something in it. I looked around, and then without hurrying I moved to that bench and sat down near the envelope. Again I looked around, but no one was taking any notice of me. With shaking hands I opened the package to find—fruit peels! Banana peels and mango peels mocked my hunger, and I started to put the envelope back on the bench.

Next moment a man was sitting beside me. He was a serious man, well dressed in a smart western suit of grey, expensive material. He was wearing a tie. I had time to notice these things as I quickly pulled my hand away from the envelope and pretended to look at something else.

"What is in the envelope?" he asked quietly, with authority.

I was frightened. Who was this person? He seemed to be someone important.

"Tell me what is in the envelope" he said again, "or else I'll hand you over to the police!" When I heard the word "police" I was very afraid, and I immediately picked up the envelope and opened it uncertainly.

The man looked and frowned. Certainly the peels did not seem worth putting into an envelope!

"What are these?" he asked. I think he had imagined that I was a member of some sort of gang and had taken delivery of this envelope containing something important. Now he looked at me with different eyes. "Are you very hungry?" he asked, compassionately. I nodded, not able to look at him for I felt ashamed.

"Come with me," he ordered. He caught me by the hand in the way of our country and drew me with him. He took me immediately to a hotel and made me sit down at a table.

"Now, what would you like?" he asked me.

"Please could I have some food?" I asked. I was famished.

"What sort of food do you want?" he asked me again, but I could not answer, so he ordered rice and *chappatis*, the flat bread of Pakistan, *biryani* and some other dishes. The table was spread like a feast day. My mouth was watering with the lovely smell of the food, and he waved me to begin. He sat watching me while I ate, but he did not ask me any questions, which was kind of him.

Afterwards, he ordered some tea for us both, and while we drank it, he asked me, "Now, what is your name? Where do you come from, and what are you doing here?"

Frankly, I did not want to tell him. But he had been so kind, and he was also a man of authority, so I decided to tell him the whole story. I don't think he really believed all that I told him, for I related the whole story of my troubles, but when I had finished he said to me, "Masood, would you like to come and work for me? I need someone to help in the house, and I think you would be happy with us. I have a wife and three children. What do you think?"

I was touched by his kind offer. It seemed to me that perhaps God had sent this man to help me at just this time, and so without further hesitation, I accepted. Besides, I reflected, did I really have any choice?

His name was Rashid, and he took me with him to his home in a nearby part of the city. After introducing his wife and children to me, he showed me a verandah with a bed where I could sleep. It was a cool place, and I was glad for this consideration. I think he felt sorry that he had misjudged me while, for my own part, I was glad that he had. Here I had a roof over my head once more, and more than that, someone who cared for my welfare. I thanked him from my heart, and he smiled at me. "The fact is, Masood, we had a servant, but the rascal has run away, and it's very unlikely that he'll be back again. You are welcome to use anything here."

In the morning I came to know more about my benefactor. He was a lawyer in the city, and his wife was a teacher. I learned over a time that he had a soft heart for boys like me that had no place to live, and previously he had been in the habit of giving them work in his home. I worked for no salary, but I was fed very well, and I felt that I was loved by this family. Once again, I reflected, God is caring for me in the most practical way. It seemed that He had not lost me after all.

I think that the lawyer felt pleased with my work for him. He said once that he had always had to watch the earlier boys very closely, but that he was glad he did not have to watch me. I suspect that he was an experienced judge of character, and he probably knew that I was very glad to be there, and that I would not do anything to make him regret his decision to take me in.

It was a well-ordered home, like most homes of this level in Pakistan. Part of my job consisted of making tea for the family in the morning. This was called bed tea, for it was brought to them first thing before they came out for food. After breakfast I would take the children to school, seeing them across the road safely, and I would meet them again in the afternoon to bring them back. This was most necessary for certain *badmashes*, bad characters, would frequent the schools, and it was not unknown for children to be kidnapped or molested. The children called me "Brother," and I was very fond of them. For the rest, my duties consisted of cleaning the house, doing the washing and going to the market to shop for fresh fruit and vegetables. It was a busy life, but not an unhappy one. I would have time off to myself in the afternoons, and I began to feel that I would be happy to do this indefinitely.

Today I wonder a little at this man's attitude to me. Certainly he taught the children to call me "Brother," but also I received no salary, and perhaps he thought that by giving me this relationship in his family I could not ask for money, though I would have been very glad of some, for I wanted to buy Islamic books to study. I was trapped by the situation even while I was quite happy in it. But I had lost my independence. I thought perhaps he would give me some money later, but it never happened.

Several months went by. I came to know Karachi and its ways well, and one day I quite unexpectedly met up with my half-brothers who lived there!

Each day I would take my employer's lunch to his office. It is the custom in some of the cities in Pakistan for servants to carry the food in a container, called a *tiffin* carrier, rather than for the worker to have to carry his own food on crowded public transport. It keeps the food fresh since it is made later, and the system works quite well. One day I was returning from the lawyer's office with the empty tiffin carrier. The bus drivers had gone on strike over a pay claim, and I was wondering what to do when along came a man in a car. He was well dressed and looked about thirty years old. He offered to take me home since he was going in my direction. He said he lived in a village some ten miles from Karachi, and along the way he dropped me off at the nearest point from which I could make my way home on foot. I thanked him warmly.

The next day he again saw me waiting for the bus and pulled up at the stop. "Where are you going today?"

I answered him, "I'm just going to take this meal to my boss in the city."

He opened the car door for me and said, "Jump in. I can take you."

I was glad to escape the crush of the bus. The strike had ended, and as always, the vehicles were crowded with people hanging out of the doors. As we went along, he asked, "How much does your boss pay you?"

This is an acceptable question in Pakistan, and I did not mind his asking me, but I had to confess that I was not paid a salary. He seemed astonished and said to me, "That's not good. Why don't you work with me, and we can earn together?"

For some reason, without thinking, I agreed.

I went home after my job was finished and told the family that I was going to work with this man I had met. I had learned that he had some sort of job selling local medicines. The lawyer was not very happy, and the children urged me not to leave them, but I was determined. After all, I had spent over nine months with them, and I did not want to work for nothing for the rest of my life. So, after about two weeks, I went to this man's village and moved into his house.

He gave me a place to sleep, and that evening I was looking around the house when, to my complete astonishment, I saw a picture of my father! It was an old photograph, but unmistakably his likeness. I was cautious though and did not say that I recognized him. I simply asked the man who it was.

"Oh," he said, "that was our father!"

This sounded like nonsense to me. I knew that their father's wife was not my mother! However, with some careful questions I found out that they were the children of one of my father's earlier marriages. It seemed that they were born a few years before I was and that they were the children of my father's third wife whom he married in about 1947, or perhaps before.

We sat and talked through much of the night. They told me the whole sad story of how my father had left their mother and gone to northern Pakistan. I took up the story and told them of his later marriage to my mother and how unhappy they were together. I thought, as we talked, of the cruelty of the Islamic system of many marriages to different women. How difficult it is for the women and how many problems it causes! The mother of my half-brothers sat listening to us talk, but she did not say very much. I felt that she was angry with me, for I represented to her what she felt was her failure as a wife to my father. One of the boys noticed this, and he said softly to her, "Mother, this one is innocent. You must not hate him."

I am sorry to say that this experiment of living with my half-brothers did not work out, and after about two months I went back to live at the house of the lawyer. They welcomed me warmly.

For one and a half years I lived there, all told. I seemed to be at a standstill. I still longed to know what God wanted for me, and I longed to know Him, but perhaps I was too comfortable. I kept up my custom of praying five times a day, and the lawyer was very impressed with my piety, but it was mostly habit. During the time of Ramadan, the strict fast of the Muslims, I was very determined to keep a total fast. The lawyer's family were Sunni Muslims, but they did not seem to mind that I was from Ahmadi background. Besides, I went faithfully to the Sunni Muslim mosque, so they could not complain.

I was very busy. I seemed to have more and more to do, and still I was not paid anything, but by this time I did not mind quite so much. I found time to go regularly to the mosque where I talked with the *imam* and others about many things, including most of the questions that had been bothering me for so many years. The imam was a good man though he was never able to give me satisfactory answers to my questions like, "Why do we do what we do?" and "Are we sure that God will accept us in paradise?" Still, in my heart, I was restless. The imam lent me many books, and I used to read these in my spare time. I think they stirred me up and made me more dissatisfied than ever.

Working in the kitchen I would stop and think, "Is this really why I left home? Is God really here?"

One night, I lay sleepless on my bed, hot with fever. My spirit was rebellious, and I kept thinking to myself, "Why bother? My life has no meaning. It looks as though God doesn't really care about me. He's playing with me, making me think that He's concerned, and then hiding Himself from me." But even as I thought these things, that sense of a Presence was again beside me, and I heard the words, "How soon you give up?"

I sat up on my bed and looked around, but there was no one there. I felt as though I had been abandoned. Soon afterwards, the lawyer called me to make tea for him and a friend who was visiting.

I dragged myself off the bed and went slowly towards the kitchen, still feeling that I wanted to be done with all this. As I passed the door of the living room, I heard a familiar voice. It was Ahmed's father! What was he doing here? Why had my friend's father come all this way from Rabwah? I paused in the doorway just out of sight, and I heard him say, "Thank you very much. His father will arrive tomorrow. But where is the boy?"

The lawyer replied, "He'll be here in a moment. He'll bring tea for us, and that will give you a chance to see him. Why don't you stand over near that cupboard, as though you were looking at my books, then he won't recognize you."

My heart hammered in my chest, and I rushed back to my quarters. I was frightened and dismayed at the sound of that voice from my past. But not knowing what else I could do, I hurried out to the kitchen and made the tea. This familiar task was comforting, and I gained control of myself. But when I brought the tea to the room, my hands were trembling.

"What's the matter, Masood?" the lawyer asked me.

I noticed out of the corner of my eye the other man standing quietly by the books. Ahmed's father had not changed much.

"Sir, I have fever," I replied, glad that it was true. He touched my hand to check and saw that I did indeed have a temperature.

"Go to my bedroom," he ordered, "and take some aspirin from the cupboard." I went out, not looking at Ahmed's father again.

My master's wife was in the bedroom reading a magazine when I called at the door. She said kindly, "Come in, Masood. What's the matter?" I told her, and she said, "You'll find the aspirin there," pointing at the cupboard. "Oh, and while you're there," will you please get me a tablet from the small bottle next to the aspirin? I must have one. I can't sleep."

I took down the bottle and did as she asked. She took a pill, several in fact, and lay down to sleep.

Her eyes were closed when I glanced across at her. I don't know what came over me, but on impulse I stuffed the bottle of sleeping pills in my pocket and slipped out of the door. She did not see me go.

Back in my little annex I sat on my bed, turning the smooth glass bottle over in my hands, counting the white pills inside, thinking how easy it would be simply to swallow them all and go to sleep forever. The idea of going to sleep forever seemed very attractive to me just then. Remembering the conversation between the lawyer and Ahmed's father, I thought of how unhappy my life was, how meaningless and false. Nobody really loved me. It seemed that they all wished to hurt me, and now my father was approaching Karachi from the north, bent on taking me back to Rabwah to punish or kill me. All around me my enemies were leering at me and saying, "Die! Die! You have no right to live. Why don't you die!"

Several times that night and into the early hours of the morning, I lifted that bottle to my mouth, thinking that I would swallow all the pills. I was not afraid of death just then, but I was afraid that after taking the pills I might somehow be revived, and then my father would be here, and I would once more be in his hands. I had to get away. I heard the neighbourhood cocks begin to crow, and the first, false light of the April dawn crept into my room. I could delay no longer. Grabbing an old briefcase that a former servant had left, I stuffed the pills and some of my personal papers into it and crept to the door. Everyone was sleeping soundly and nobody saw me. Opening the door, I slipped through into the garden, and within moments I was out in the main road. Here I was, almost twenty years old; I had no family, no job and apparently no future on earth and beyond, as another chapter of my life drew to a close.

9

Beyond Suicide

I wandered in the cool of the early morning as the city awoke to another day. My life seemed utterly futile, and the thought that my father would soon be in Karachi filled me with despair. I thought again of that little bottle of white pills in the briefcase I was carrying with me, and a searing voice in my brain kept saying to me, "End it all. Go to sleep, sleep. ..."

Around ten o'clock I found myself at one of the many temporary restaurants that spring up in Pakistan wherever there is a need for them. This one catered for the many construction laborers who would come and drink tea and have their meals there. It was set on a vacant piece of land, surrounded by buildings, and as I sat down alone I reflected that this was a very ordinary place to end my life! For that is what I had determined to do by this time, and as I ordered tea I opened the briefcase and took out the bottle of pills. As I looked at them again it seemed to me that death itself was mocking me. For a moment I hesitated, while the tea was brought with the customary glass of water; then I made up my mind and turned my thoughts from the fear that perhaps I might not die. I had absolutely no idea of what might be waiting for me beyond death, but I knew that I just wanted to escape this life.

Without hesitating any longer, I opened the bottle and emptied the entire contents into my mouth, swallowing the pills with the glass of water. I had a brief moment of panic, then deliberately drank the tea. I fumbled in the briefcase for a piece of paper, and with a pencil I wrote: "I am desperate. There is no way out for me. I have decided to leave this world. I know that God is somewhere, but since He does not care about me there is nothing else to do."

I signed my name to this sad little note, put it in my pocket, paid for the tea and walked out. I intended that when I died, they would find it on my body and at least someone would know what had happened. But first, I wanted to get to a deserted place where no one would find me and make me go to a doctor.

As I crossed the road, it seemed to me that the buildings were doing a drunken dance as the pills began to take effect. I understood what was happening, but I was worried that, like a wounded animal, I had still not found a place to die. I turned down another street, looking to the right and to the left, but there was nowhere to lie down. The street was wide with trees growing down its length, and on both sides the high-walled bungalows told me that I was in a wealthy area where I would be very lucky to find anywhere. The guards at the gates of some of the houses, the *chowkidars* looked at me with suspicion, thinking perhaps that I had come to look over the houses that I would like to rob.

By the time I reached the corner, I could not stand upright. Quickly I clung to a telephone pole, and I heard a voice asking me kindly, "What's the matter? Not feeling well?"

I turned my face to the voice and noticed on the roof of a nearby house a kind-faced woman. It was nice to have someone concerned for me, but it was too late now. She spoke again, "I think it must be this hot weather why you're not feeling well. Please come inside for a while."

She made her way down from the roof, and I heard the door open as she came to unlock the gate. I was really frightened now and just wanted to leave, but I could not move. My legs felt like cooked rice. I tried to walk, and for a moment I thought I was walking on air. Then there was darkness, and I knew no more.

When I opened my eyes again the world was full of shadows. I had a vague idea that I had come to the next world, but as my mind cleared, I realized that I was in a cool room, and that there were women and children there. Then I saw the doctor sitting by the bed. He smiled when I looked at him and gave me a big bowl of water, "Here, old chap, drink this."

I tried, for he seemed a good man, but I could not manage it. So he asked the others to leave the room. Another man came from the head of the bed, apparently his assistant, and he held me while the doctor inserted a rubber tube down my throat to wash out my stomach. I gagged and wished wholeheartedly that I had died! I didn't realize then that the doctor must have known what I had done.

It only took fifteen minutes, but to me it seemed like fifteen hours! Then the man gave me an injection and invited the women to come back. They had been waiting outside, it seemed, and eagerly trooped back into the room to see their unexpected patient and guest. It was then that I recalled the face of the kind woman who had invited me in, and I realized that I must be in her house. The children clustered around her, shrilly talking about me. They called her *"Api,"* She warmly thanked the doctor for coming and he said, "I wouldn't have done this for anyone else. If this boy had died, I would have lost my medical license. This should be a police case."

Only then did I realize that these people had taken a considerable risk for me, and I felt warmth and thankfulness towards them all. The doctor took his leave shortly afterwards, and I was left lying in a strange bed among strangers.

For a while they plied me with questions, but I am afraid I was too sleepy from the injection to answer them clearly. I was dimly aware of a man's voice, but I did not see his face. And then I slept. ...

When I awoke it was getting dark, and I felt much better. My head was clear, and I was able to take note of my surroundings. I was lying in a large cool room, tastefully furnished, and the thought came to me that perhaps God had allowed me to begin to die on the doorstep of these kind people so that they might find me and restore me. It was a good thought, and whereas before I had longed for death, I now gave thanks for life.

Since I felt so much better I got up off the bed. Two men, hearing me, came in and introduced themselves. One of them was the owner of the house, Mr. Qureshi, and I thanked him warmly for his kindness and goodness to me. He smiled when I asked him when I should leave and said that we would talk of that later.

"For the time being, Masood, you must stay and get better. If you are all right, perhaps you can leave tomorrow."

That night we talked for many hours. I told the Qureshis much of my sad story, and I heard the others talking about me in hushed voices as the story was passed around the house. When I spoke of my searching for the true God and His followers, they were astonished. The women put their hands to their faces and spoke rapidly to each other. I think it must have been that which decided Mr. Qureshi, for he spoke to me before we went to bed. "Masood, our home is open to you. We will be glad to have you here, and you can stay as one of our own children. We are Muslims, and we are proud of it because the truth is Islam, as you will discover. Only Islam can bring you joy and satisfaction. Here you can forget your pagan [Ahmadi] background, and here you will discover the truth."

He looked very pleased as he said this, and *Api* [Mrs. Qureshi] agreed with him.

"That's right, Masood. You must search with faith and diligence and not be afraid. You're lucky that here God has shown you the true way to life. You have come out from among the pagans, and there will be no boundaries to your research here. And now, let's all get to bed. It's quite late."

A boy servant showed me to my room. I had been moved from the place where I had been lying before, and for a moment I stood at the doorway, amazed. I thought I must be dreaming. The room was like a luxury hotel to me. It had a soft bed and a table where I could read and write. It even had a bathroom en suite. Once more my thoughts flew to God. How unpredictable He was! Before, I had almost been a dead dog on the road; now I was living in comfort and luxury, beginning a new life. ...

In the cupboard along one wall, I noticed to my joy a number of books. Quickly, I crossed the room and bent to look at the titles. They were all Islamic books, expensively bound. Qur'anic commentaries jostled with books on the Hadith, and there were more volumes of biography and many other titles besides. I rejoiced at the thought of spending hours studying them. My eyes filled with tears, and in my heart I said a prayer of thanksgiving that the all-wise God had not let me die, but had introduced me to a whole new life.

Next day I was up with the dawn. I bathed in my own bathroom, and the black thoughts of the day before had all gone. I prayed the obligatory prayer and recited several chapters of the Qur'an in thanks to God. I ate with the family, and after Mr. Qureshi had gone to work, his wife said to me, "Today, Masood, you must come with me to the bazaar. We must get you some new clothes if you're going to stay here with us."

I was touched by her kindness, and the thought crossed my mind that this, too, was God's doing. When He is kind to us, the whole world becomes kind. When God honors someone, no one can dishonor him. I could not understand it, but what I did understand was that, for some reason, God had begun to look upon me kindly, and now He was showing me how much He cared for me. Then another more disturbing thought touched me: He had really been kind to me all along, but only now was I beginning to understand His ways! I followed Mrs. Qureshi, dazed with happiness. Everywhere in the crowded noisy bazaar, people seemed to smile on me. When the shopkeepers understood that I was with this good woman, they took special care to please her. By the time we returned home, I felt that I was clothed like a king.

I was accepted by the Qureshis from the start. No one objected to my research, and everyone was kind and helpful. Today, when I think about that time, I thank God that He provided for me, step by step, just what I needed. Clearly, what I required then was a stable, loving environment to pursue Him, and in that home I found it.

In Rabwah, I had really only read Ahmadi books. Even the Qur'anic commentaries I read in those early days were written with an Ahmadi bias. Now I had the opportunity to study from the other side, and I made the most of that time. Every day I spent long hours at the desk in my room studying, comparing, analyzing, making notes. In the evenings I would often discuss my research with Mr. Qureshi, and I found him to be a learned man, though very dogmatic. He was a banker and a man of good repute. Seeing my interest and dedication, he introduced me to some reputable Muslim scholars like Mawlana Ihtisham al-Haq, Fazl ur-Rahman Ansari and Mawlana Abul A'la Mawdudi. I felt so honored sitting in their company listening to them and their audience for hours. And although these discussions did not answer several of my key questions about life in this world and in the hereafter, all the time, my heart was being drawn to God yearning to know Him.

Several months passed. The Qureshis accepted me completely and even loved me. They would not even allow me to work in the house to help pay them for all their many kindnesses to me.

"Oh, no, Masood," said *Api*. "You're welcome to stay as long as you like to study the truths of Islam. There are others who can work for us, and besides, you are more a son to us than a servant." And she smiled at me kindly as she said it.

One day, Mr. Qureshi called me to speak with him. "We have completed our enquiries about you, Masood," he began, and as he said this my heart sank. Did this mean I would have to leave? I waited painfully for him to continue. "I've warned your parents, Masood, that if they have wronged you, they will have to face the consequences. I hope you don't mind my speaking to them this way, but I thought it best for your future."

I could breathe again! He noticed my tenseness and reached out to touch my arm. "That's very good of you, Sir," I said. "And now, if you don't mind, I'd like to find a little job for myself."

He frowned at that. "What's the matter, Masood? Do you need money?"

"It's not that so much," I replied slowly. "I'd like to stand on my own feet and not be a burden to you."

I think he appreciated my desire to be independent, and his voice was warm when he said, "OK then, Masood. That's settled. I'll find a job for you."

+ + + + +

In my study on Islam I was very much drawn toward Mawlana Mawdudi's writings. Among many of his books, I treasured his commentary on the Qur'an. His arguments and reasons were powerful, but still somehow I was unable to find answers to my dilemma concerning whether I was following the right path and if by following Islamic rules and rituals God would accept me in His paradise. That quest seemed a long way off.

It was indeed interesting to know that Mawdudi's *Jama'at-e-Islami* has been one of the main religious organizations which since 1953 actively demanded of the government of Pakistan that Ahmadiyya Muslims should be declared non-Muslims because of their non-Islamic beliefs and practices, but it was in 1974 it achieved the goal.

Whenever Mawlana's visit to Karachi was adver- tised, I tried my best to attend his lectures. At times my inquisitiveness would persuade me to attend some of his organization's conferences at Mansorah in Lahore. Due to so many trying to have audience with him, our conversations were always short. He would recommend some of his or other classical scholars' writings to me to find my answers.

In that year, 1971, tensions between India and Paki- stan over the status of East Pakistan came to a head, leading to war in December and the setting up of the state of Bangladesh. For many months before this, there was great strain in the city, and people went about with concerned faces, aware that there would be fighting before long. I went off to work regularly, and all my spare time was spent in study and dialogue with Islamic scholars to whom Mr. Qureshi had kindly introduced me.

As the year lengthened into winter the fighting began in earnest. Almost every night there would be air raids, and the sirens would sound, sending everyone scuttling for shelter.

One night I sat under the stairs at the house, listening to the "crump" of the bombs not far away. The Indian fliers seemed to be very courageous, I thought, and I stuck my fingers in my ears to block out the sound of the explosions. As usual, I was praying and from time to time reciting the familiar passages from the Qur'an in Arabic. On this occasion I was reciting the traditional creed, *Iman-Mofasil*, the Exposition of Faith, and for once I stopped after each phrase to ask myself about the words of the familiar cadences.

"*Amantu bil-laah*, I believe in God," I recited aloud. "Is it really so?" I asked myself. "Do I really believe?" In my soul I knew that I did believe, and I passed on to the next part of the text.

"... and his angels," I said. "Of course I believe in them."

"... and his books. Yes," I said with conviction as I recalled the creed from my schooldays.

"But you also believe that they are corrupted and only the Qur'an is intact." I seemed to ask myself, "How can you believe in the Torah, the Injil and the books given to prophets before Muhammad if they are corrupted? ..."

As the sounds of the air raid died away in the distance and the sirens sounded the all-clear, I thought further about all this. I came out from the safety of the staircase, my mind full of deep thoughts, and made my way to my room. There, before I turned on the light, I covered the windows with blankets so the light could not be seen in the event of another raid, and only then did I lay down on my bed. But I could not rest, so I got up and switched on the table lamp, covering it with a towel so the light was directed onto my desk. Sitting down, I opened the Qur'an.

Idly I turned the pages at random, and there it was written:

O, ye who believe: Believe in Allah and His Messenger and the Scripture which He hath revealed unto His Messenger and the Scripture which He hath revealed aforetime. Whoso disbelieveth in Allah and His angels and His Scriptures and His Mesengers and the Last

Day, he verily hath wandered far astray (Sura 4 verse 136).

I remembered another passage, and after turning a few pages back I found how the Qur'an expected that we as Muslims should declare the following:

> We believe in Allah and that which is revealed unto us and that which was revealed unto Ibrahim (Abraham) and Ismail (Ishmael) and Ishaq (Isaac) and Yaqub (Jacob) and the tribes and that which was given to Musa (Moses) and Isa (Jesus) and the prophets from their Lord. We make no distinction between any of them and unto Him we have surrendered (Sura 3 verse 84).

I paused at these words, my heart racing. What did they mean? I knew that it was because of the word of God that I had first got into trouble with my own people back in Rabwah. They said they believed God's Scriptures, but in fact they did not really want to believe them all. For all practical purposes they held that some of these things just did not apply. That night I came to know, beyond doubt, that God had said that these books, books that included the *Injil*, were a "light and guidance for mankind" (Sura 6 verse 92; Sura 40 verse 53) and that they were "the clear Scripture" (Sura 37 verse 117). Then, what of the word in Sura 5 verse 46, "We bestowed on Him [Jesus] wherein is guidance and a light, confirming that which was [revealed] before in the Torah—a guidance and an admonition unto those who ward off evil?"

The air-raid siren interrupted my feverish thoughts, and reluctantly I turned off the light. Sitting on the chair in the dark I thought of how many times I had recited those words like a trained parrot, but today when I concentrated on them, the words of these verses touched my conscience to the depths. Suddenly, I had a great desire to read the Bible again, to start with a new attitude, a new beginning. Yes, I was aware that they said it had been corrupted and changed. I knew some Muslim scholars had warned me that studying the Bible would corrupt and dissolve my faith. But in my heart I knew differently.

If my faith was worth anything at all, then it would survive. It was not like a piece of brittle sandstone that would crack and shatter into a thousand pieces if it was dropped! If you really trust the true God, I told myself seriously, then you will be all right. There and then I resolved to read and study the subject further for myself. I would compare the Qur'an and the Bible.

After all, I reasoned as the anti-aircraft guns resumed their lethal barking, if the Qur'an admonishes me to have faith in the Bible, then clearly it could not have been changed in Muhammad's time. If I say that it was changed afterwards, then I am really disobeying God and refusing to believe Him. After all, if God knew that His word would be changed later, He would never have endorsed it in the first place. Or so I reasoned.

In any case, I was determined to get hold of a Bible again.

10

The Bible and the Qur'an

When I awoke the very next day, my first thought was to get hold of a Bible. It seemed to me that the best place to ask for one would be the church where I went when I first arrived in Karachi—St Andrew's Church of Scotland.

After breakfast, I made my way there eagerly, hoping that I would meet someone who would help me. However, I was disappointed, for when I arrived there, the place was locked up, and I did not have the courage to go and look for someone. Disconsolately I wandered on down the road until I saw on my right, yet another church, the Central Methodist Church. My immediate thought was that I would be able to get a Bible here, and I did not hesitate, but went in through the open gate.

Three or four people were standing and chatting near the church hall, and as I approached them they fell silent. I think they knew I was a Muslim, and they did not appear very friendly. I greeted them, however, and said to the nearest man, "Please, can you help me to get a Bible?"

The men just looked at me, and one of them said, "Why don't you go to the Bible Society. They'll give you one."

This was the first time I had heard of the society, and I asked the man for the address. He told me where to go, but it was in an unfamiliar part of Karachi, and I did not want to wait any longer for my Bible.

"Could you please lend me a Bible then?" I asked hopefully. "When I've read it I can return it to you."

The man who had spoken earlier was unfriendly.

"If you really want to read it, you can buy one. You're like the rest of them. They all want to read, but none of them want to buy."

I was surprised by his attitude.

"I can give you the money," I said, a bit stiffly. As I spoke, two other men approached, and I heard the conversation. One of them mocked me, "Oh, Reverend, do give him a Bible," he said, though I could see that he was not serious. For some reason the men now listened to me seriously, and I told them at length why I wanted to have a Bible. The pastor, for that is who one of the men was, spoke more kindly and asked me my name.

"Come with me, friend, and we can talk in my office."

He invited me to sit down, and I told him more of my quest. He listened attentively, and there was no hesitation when I once more asked for a Bible. He took one from his cupboard and held it in his hands and said, "Masood, guard this book. It is the word of life."

I took it thankfully and offered to pay for it, but he shook his head.

"The word of life is free to all who seek it truly," he said gently as he stood up. "Take it and read it carefully, Masood, and it will water your soul."

I held the Bible to my chest thankfully, only half hearing as the other man in the room, an elderly gentleman, invited me to the worship service the following

Sunday afternoon. I said that I would come and bid them both goodbye.

That evening we heard on the news that there was to be a ceasefire, and hearts everywhere were filled with thankfulness. However, the black-out restrictions were still in force, and before I sat down to read my new Bible, I carefully checked the blankets at the window and the towel over the lamp. And then I began.

I opened the book reverently and began at Genesis. The first words of the opening chapter riveted my attention. Here was the same creation work of God, the same calling of light and so on. "It's the same as it is in the Qur'an," I thought, remembering the words: "When He ordaineth a thing, He saith unto it only, Be, and it is."

That night I stayed up studying much longer than usual, fascinated by the things I read. When I finally closed the book, my eyes were burning and my mind racing as I lay down on my bed to sleep. The procession of patriarchs marched before me, it seemed. The same prophets who were mentioned in the Bible were familiar to me from the years of reading the Qur'an. The same Noah, Abraham and Lot. The same Ishmael, Isaac, Jacob and Joseph. The same story of Moses before Pharaoh. The same Aaron ...

The same David who sang (or as Muslims may say he recited) the *Zabur,* the lovely psalms ... The same Solomon who was given wisdom and knowledge ...

The same job, and even Jonah ...

To me that night, it seemed that the whole of the Old Testament was like a commentary on the Qur'an.

The next few days were spent in avid study of the Bible. The Qureshis noticed that I spent more time in my room and were a little disturbed, though they said nothing then. By this time, several important things were becoming clear to me. For instance, Islam teaches that the prophets lived totally holy and innocent lives, but the more I read the Bible, the more I saw that they were presented in quite a different light—as mortal men, subject to the weaknesses and frailties of the flesh of mankind. It was strange to me to see written down: the lustful sin of David, the way that Jeremiah shouted against God, and the disobedience of Moses. I was quite shocked that these things should be written about so frankly, and yet I was encouraged. If these men were as weak as I and yet God used them …? And so I read on.

As I reflected on these things, I alternated between feeling that it should not have been written like this and feeling that this in itself was a testimony of the truth. One part of me cried out, "It's blasphemy!" And once or twice I even closed the Bible for a while before I could take it out to read again. But inside me there was a quiet voice saying, "If these books have been changed, why didn't the Israelites remove these same stories since they are so proud of their ancestors? Why are those stories still there?" Surely this was significant.

With this thought, I looked at the Qur'an again to see whether there was anything about forgiveness in connection with the lives of the prophets and the patriarchs. To my surprise, there was! According to the Qur'an, many of these men of God did sin and asked God's forgiveness for it. For example, Adam, one could read of in Sura 7 verses 23 and 24, Noah, in Sura II verse 47, Abraham, in Sura 14 verses 40 and 41. Likewise Moses, in Sura 28 verse 16 and David, Sura 38 verses 23 and 24.

I felt this was a remarkable thing, since Muslims everywhere held them all to be sinless.

By this time, the Qureshis had become concerned about my studies. One evening Mrs. Qureshi spoke to me. "Masood," she said gently, "you must realize that much study is weariness to the flesh. You should get out more."

I thanked her and said that my studies were coming along well. She was not satisfied with my reply and said, "Masood, you should compare the lives of Muhammad and Jesus. Then you will soon see that our Muhammad is the real one to follow and that he alone is the blessing to the world."

That Sunday, remembering my promise to the old man at the Central Methodist Church, I made my way to the worship meeting in the afternoon. When I arrived, the meeting was just about to begin, and I slipped into the back row quietly. The service did not mean very much to me, though I was impressed at the place given to Jesus, whom they all addressed as Lord and Savior. Part of me rebelled against this, but another part of me found it very peaceful and helpful.

The preacher noticed me at the back of the church, and afterwards he spoke to me warmly. His name was Mr. Vincent, and with him was Mr. Massey, the gentleman who had invited me to the worship. Mr. Vincent asked me to join him in his office, and I accepted.

We chatted together for a long time. I was full of questions and asked if I might speak of them. Mr. Vincent nodded.

"In the Qur'an," I began, "we find the doctrine of the birth, teaching, miracles and ascension of Jesus, but there is nothing about the terms 'Father' and 'Son.' Of course, the Qur'an says, 'He begetteth not, nor was begotten ...'"

Mr. Vincent watched my face as I spoke, then he said to me, "That's right, Masood. In the Qur'an God has an important name—'*Al-wadood*' One who takes care in love—but the *Injil*, the gospel, does not say so much that He loves, but that He is Love itself. In other words, His name is not only *Al-wadood*, but He is *Al-wadood* personified."

"Our Bible uses the terms Father and Son to restore the relationship between God and humanity. On the other hand, Islam believes only that God is Lord and that we are all His servants. But the gospel, the *Injil*, says about Jesus, 'God so loved the world, that he gave his only begotten Son [Jesus], that whosoever believeth in him should not perish, but have everlasting life' (John 3:16)."

"That is precisely my problem," I butted in. "How can it be that Jesus Christ is the Son of God?"

Mr. Vincent smiled at my eagerness.

"Well, Masood, it's a spiritual relationship that we're, talking about, and you must keep that clearly in mind. It has nothing at all to do with fleshly birth, and this is something that Muslims apparently cannot and will not understand: We're talking of spiritual relationships.

"Let me try to illustrate this, Masood. When we call Muhammad Ali Jinnahu as 'The Father of our Nation,' does this mean that the whole nation of Pakistan has actually sprung from his loins? Of course not! And likewise, we Christians believe, 'His Son, Jesus Christ our Lord, which was made of the seed of David according to the flesh; and declared to be the Son of God with power, according to the spirit of holiness, by the resurrection from the dead'" (Romans 1:3-4).

His face shone as he spoke these wonderful words, and I could see how much this all meant to him.

"But," he continued, "Christ is called 'the Word of God' and 'the Spirit of God' according to the Qur'an and these terms are used in the Bible too, where he is also called 'Son.'

"When we believe that God is eternal, so His Word clearly must also be eternal and Christ is the Word and Spirit of God. This obviously means that Jesus is also eternal, and we are forced to believe in the deity of Jesus Christ. He is indeed the eternal."

He stopped, and I was left speechless. I had never seen it so clearly before, nor had I heard an exposition like this before. I had heard so many times what the Muslims said of Jesus, but this was the first time I had heard it so clearly put from the Christian point of view. Once more, I found myself torn by the arguments I was hearing. All my Muslim heritage urged me to reject this reasoning, but my heart was warmed and drawn by it just the same. The words of a poet which someone had jokingly quoted to me once came to my mind so clearly: "When he reads the *Injil,* a Muslim turns from Islam."

I wondered if this could be happening to me! ...

Mr. Vincent seemed to sense my distress, for he did not press me. Rather he asked if I had any other questions just then. I shook my head slowly, feeling intensely that somehow the central pillar of my Islamic fort had been broken down.

"If you don't mind, sir," I said, "I will ask my other questions another time. First I must study more about these things, and then I will come again."

He stood up and came round from the other side of his desk.

"I quite understand," he said. "I'll be glad to see you here anytime."

For the next few days which turned into weeks I spent much time discussing these things that I had heard at the church with Muslim scholars, but the strength of Mr. Vincent's powerful words stayed with me, and I could not forget them. My further appointments with Mawlana Mawdudi did not materialize due to his ill health and I not being able to travel to Lahore to visit him or his right hand Mawlana Tufail at Mansorah, Lahore.

Among others I met scholars like Mawlana Banuri at his *Dar al-Uloom* and especially Mawlana Fazlur Rahman, the leader of the Centre of the World Islamic Federation in Karachi. They were not easy people to meet when the chat was to be on comparative religion and on Islam and Christianity or Muhammad and Jesus in particular. At both centers I was given literature and books like *Masihiyyat Kiya Hai* – What is Christianity? Other books like *Izharul-Haqq*, originally written in the 19th century by a Rahmatullah Kayranwi but now edited by a Mawlana Muhammad Taqqi with the new title in Urdu, *Bible say Qur'an tak*.

Mawlana Fazlur Rahman was always very busy. But one evening after prayers, I visited him with several letters and references. He seemed to have had too many things on his mind, and we were interrupted so much by others. On the other hand I was not impressed with his arguments. It seemed he was not interested in my spiritual well-being.

"Do you believe that God is the Creator?" he asked me abruptly.

"Yes, indeed, God is the Creator."

"Then," he continued, "if you want to be a true Muslim there can be no question about God. But what of Muhammad? Do you believe in Muhammad, that he is the Prophet of God and that he is the blessed one for this world and the hereafter and that Islam is the true religion?"

This barrage of questions hit me. He had already made it clear that there could be no real discussion about these things, only belief. "Sir," I asked, "are you saying I must believe blindly?" "Well, even in Christianity you must have blind faith," he retorted. "That may be," I said, "but there is so much evidence in Christianity for those things. What I am asking for is evidence for the Muslim belief."

The dogmas rolled over me like a wave. I must believe, believe, he insisted. Believe in the five pillars of Islam; don't question what has been received. There was nothing for my heart to be glad in; the whole argument was to my mind, and that was not helpful. Anything I said, especially regarding the biblical views on the Trinity, Sonship of Jesus Christ, etc., he would not even listen to.

Finally, I excused myself and got up to go. He was just about ready to throw me out by this time anyway. He thrust some articles at me (several he had written himself) and told me I should read them carefully. They were all about how Christianity had been changed and perverted, and to be honest, they looked as dry as the dust on the road. However, I was resolved to do one thing: to study carefully the lives of both Jesus and Muhammad and to compare them. I remembered Mrs. Qureshi's words to me, and it seemed that it was time for me to act on them.

The next evening, I opened my Bible at random and read these words:

"And many other signs truly did Jesus in the presence of his disciples, which are not written in this book: But these are written, that ye might believe that Jesus is the Christ, the Son of God; and that believing ye might have life through his name" (John 20:30-31).

These words seemed to have been written specifically for my need, but again the deity of Jesus stuck in my throat, and I could not easily accept it. Miracles, Faith, Eternal life! What sort of man was Jesus Christ, I wondered. More than ever, I resolved that I would study this great life and see where it led me. I knew that the Qur'an mentioned the miracles of Jesus, though they were not always the ones that the Bible mentioned. The *Hadith* speaks of Muhammad turning the moon into two pieces, though it also speaks of his healing the sick and of his multiplying food for his disciples, etc. Were the miracles of Jesus any different from those that Muhammad was supposed to have done, I wondered? But the Qur'an definitely stated that Muhammad did not perform miracles! Did Muslims feel bound to say that he did in order to counter the claims of Jesus?

My mind went to verse 7 in Sura 13 where it is written: "Those who disbelieve say, 'If only some portent were sent down upon him from his Lord. Thou art a warner only.'"

And further, in Sura 29 verse 50 it is said of Muhammad: "And they say, 'Why are not portents [miracles] sent down upon him from his Lord?' Say *portents are with Allah only* and I am but a plain warner." In other words, the Prophet Muhammad never claimed to do miracles. But it was clear that miracles were as natural to Jesus as breathing! I was uneasy as I thought this over.

Only God could do miracles. Christ did miracles. Did I dare to draw the logical conclusion—that Christ was God?

My heart trembled in prayer: "O, Creator God, show me the straight path, the path of those whom thou hast favored, not the path of those who earn thine anger nor of those who go astray." I wept as I prayed these words from my heart.

At that moment I felt as though someone was in the room, and that He wanted to say something to me. I looked around eagerly, but there was no one there that I could see. Yet ... yet someone, something, was calling to me. I looked down at my Bible where it lay open on the desk and took it up. It was open at a different place to the one where I had been reading. With disbelieving eyes I read these words:

"Ask, and it shall be given you ... For every one that asketh, receiveth, and he that seeketh findeth; and to him that knocketh it shall be opened" (Matthew 7:7-8).

God had spoken to me! It was He who had led me to these words. I trembled as I realized that He had accepted my prayer and that He had given me the answer.

For the next week I continued to study the miracles recorded in the Bible. I found that there was a great difference between those of the Hebrew prophets and those of Jesus Christ. It seemed to me that the prophets used the power for their own benefit quite often whereas Jesus did not.

For example, when Elijah spoke to the widow of Zarephath: "Make me thereof a little cake first, and bring it unto me, and after make for thee and for thy son" (I Kings 17:13). And clearly the prophets used God's power at times in drastic ways (2 Kings 1:9-14).

But Jesus, though he had all power from God, did not call His angels to save His life and to destroy His enemies. The prophets would say, "God says this. ..." But Jesus always said, "Truly, truly, I say unto you. ... Muhammad said of himself:

"Say, I am only a mortal like you. My Lord inspireth in me that your God is only one God. And whoever hopeth for the meeting with his Lord, let him do righteous work and make none sharer of the worship unto his Lord" (Sura 18 verse 110).

Jesus spoke consistently of Himself. "Come unto me, all ye that labor and are heavy laden, and I will give you rest" (Matthew 11:28); "I and my father are one" (John 10:30); "I am the way, the truth, and the life; no man cometh unto the father, but by me" (John 14:6).

Of Muhammad, who was called "*A Mercy for the Universe,*" Muslims knew that he said of himself—"I have no power to hurt or benefit myself, save that which Allah willeth" (Sura 10 verse 49).

But Jesus the Christ said: "All power is given unto me. ..." (Matthew 28:18).

This was utterly perplexing and strange to me. Here is the Prophet Muhammad who has the name of one who brings all blessing for the universe, but with what power does he bestow it? He was only mortal like us, I thought, and his tomb is there for all Muslims to see. He cannot save us. On the other hand, Jesus, to whom Islam gives only very limited authority, can say of Himself. "I am the resurrection, and the life ..." (John 11:25).

On the one hand, the Prophet of Islam sleeps forever in a tomb in Medina, but the tomb in Jerusalem, which

Jesus occupied for three days, is empty, and many saw Him literally taken up into heaven.

The Prophet Muhammad symbolizes security and peace to millions. But he himself needs our prayers and petitions. Five times daily, devout Muslims the world over pray to Allah for peace for their Prophet!

It was clear that I was coming to a point of decision. The *mawlawis* to whom I took my problems had no answers. They only became angry and threatened to throw me out. And yet I had no intention of being disruptive; I just wanted to know. And I am sure now that there are thousands and thousands of Muslims in the world who are just as I was then, with a real desire to know the truth.

11

Light in a Dark Place

Mr. Massey was a gentle man with grey hair. He lived alone and was always happy to see me. On this particular day he greeted me lovingly, and I sat in the kitchen as he prepared tea for us both. When it was ready we walked together to the lounge and sat quietly, sipping the scalding sweet liquid.

On a table nearby, I noticed a little booklet and picked it up. It was entitled, *Najat* – Salvation, and I opened it and read a few pages while Mr. Massey watched me. Something in the tract prompted me to ask him, "Muslims believe that righteousness and faith in Allah, plus our good deeds, will save us. Is this the same as Christianity?" Mr. Massey shook his head. "No, Masood. We Christians believe that 'All have sinned, and come short of the glory of God.' We cannot save ourselves by works of righteousness, for there is only one name under heaven by which we can be saved. Of course, that is Jesus our Lord. God's mercy and grace is available through Him. He is the only way to know the grace of God that brings salvation."

He said a number of other things as well that day, things that rang true with me. I felt that I was getting good answers to my questions, and we talked for a long time.

Mr. Massey had really experienced the truth of what he told me. He had originally come from India to Pakistan at the time of the Partition in 1947 and had for many years worked in an arms depot. Later, he moved to Karachi to work, and he had been there ever since. He had known much loneliness and sorrow in his life. His wife had died some years before, and it seems that they had had a number of children, but none of them had lived. Yet on this man's face the brightness of faith in the Lord Jesus shone, and I understood that he knew very well the truth of the things of which he spoke.

As I got up to leave, I asked him if I could borrow a few books that compared Islamic and Christian doctrines, but regrettably he had none. "It's very hard to find books like that in Pakistan today. There have been many such books written, but today our government does not allow such books to be published. People found in possession of them can be heavily fined."

This was the first time I had heard of such a thing, and it surprised me, for until then, I had the idea that in such matters a person was free to follow his own inclination and study what he liked, especially concerning religion. However, Mr. Massey was able to lend me some books of Christian doctrine, and we walked to the door together.

As I was about to leave, he placed his hand on my head in blessing and said, "May God bless you, my son."

At home Mr. Qureshi was waiting for me. He had some good news for me about a permanent job. He told me that he had discovered some vacancies in the Postal Services and that I should complete an application form without delay. I was very pleased.

"Thank you very much, Apa," I stammered, and he smiled at my pleasure.

"You should send the form in immediately, Masood," he urged, and gave me the address. "Now come and have your food or it will be cold."

Everyone was in a good mood. Mrs. Qureshi looked at me and observed, "Masood, these days you always seem to be eating with Christians. When you come and eat with us you must be sure to wash carefully and recite the *Kalima* at the same time, so you don't bring any pollution to the table."

She was half serious, I knew, but I turned it into a joke.

"Api, I don't think you go far enough." She looked surprised, and I picked up a side plate and turned it over to look at the maker's stamp on the bottom.

"You know, of course, that these plates are made in the People's Republic of China. They are communists and are far worse than Christians, for they are not People of the Book at all. I think we should all recite the entire Holy Qur'an before we eat off these dishes; don't you agree?"

And they all roared with laughter.

It was in February 1972 that I received word from the Postal Services Division that I had been accepted to begin work with them. Before being appointed, I underwent three months' training and my studies suffered as a result. But by the time I began my regular duties, I found myself free at the end of the eight-hour work day and was able to resume my reading.

In this way, I read almost the entire stock of Christian books that various friends lent me. I would like to have been able to read when I had nothing to do at work, but of course, this was impossible. The work was relatively undemanding and was mostly supervisory in nature. Along with other trainees, I had had to learn postal districts, regions and codes, how to check that the mail had not been tampered with, how to check that nothing was being smuggled in and so on. It was a responsible job, but to me the hours tended to drag until I was free to go home and resume the studies that were so important to me.

One evening I was studying the subject of sin and its beginnings. It struck me that nowhere in the Qur'an did one find that Jesus sinned, and of course, in the Bible He could ask of His enemies, "Which of you convinceth me of sin?" (John 8:46).

It is also true that the Qur'an does not speak of the sinfulness of Muhammad, though there are a number of verses, such as Sura 110 verse 3 which says, "Then hymn the praises of the Lord and seek forgiveness of Him. Lo, He is ever ready to show mercy."

And elsewhere, in Sura 48 verses 1 and 2 the Qur'an says,

> Lo, we have given thee a signal victory that Allah may forgive thee of thy sin that is past and that is to come and may perfect His favor unto thee and may guide thee on a right path.

Looking at these verses I was struck by the apparent difference that existed between the teaching of Islam today—that Muhammad was without sin—and the revelation of the Qur'an.

It was clear to me by then, too, that Jesus had a radically different idea about women than that taught by Islam. It was amazing how He protected the rights of women. His teaching about divorce, for example, in Matthew 5:31 and 32 was completely different from that expressed by Islam. Whereas Jesus protected wives by His teaching, the Qur'an teaches something very different:

> As for those of your women who are guilty of lewd-ness, call to witness four of you against them. And if they testify, then confine them to the house until death take them or Allah appoint for them a way (Sura 4 verse 15).

If this was the famous "equality" given to Muslim women, then I thought that the Christian way was much superior! Islam, in practice, clearly gives prefer-ence to men, while women are more like pieces of prop-erty. Even in paradise, according to the Qur'an there are no joys to be expected for women believers. The men have much to look forward to—much of it apparently immoral—but for women the Qur'an is silent. I found myself rebelling against this unequal philosophy that kept women in such bondage to men.

I sat silently in my chair, thinking. Just then, as I watched, the breeze took the pages of my Bible and blew them gently, and to my astonishment, they opened to a passage that exactly spoke to my heart:

> Come out of her, my people, that ye be not partakers of her sins, and that ye receive not of her plagues. For her sins have reached unto heaven, and God hath remembered her iniquities (Revelation 18:4-5).

Reading these words I trembled inwardly. What should I do? I could not even pray.

On the one side was the Muslim teaching about paradise and against that were Jesus' simple words:

> For when they shall rise from the dead, they neither marry, nor are given in marriage; but are as the angels which are in heaven (Mark 12:25).

It seemed to me that those people who held Islam to be a complete system of law and order for all of life were mistaken. They cry that Islam has freed women. But was that the real freedom that God intended for women whom He had made? Remembering that Muslim women have no right to divorce their husbands, but can themselves be divorced by the three-fold repetition of the formula "I divorce you." I felt angry that this should be so. I felt like crying in the street: "Oh, people of Islam, go and see the divorced women in our Muslim society. See the women who are now spending their days in their parents' houses. See them in the streets, begging and prostituting themselves, for they have no one to care for them. See the children's anguish and need. See them, people of Islam: those kicked out of their homes by their husbands, unable to live decently and rightly because they are not accepted. Look at them and be ashamed for our Islamic society! See those women whose husbands have married many wives and who cannot support them properly. Is this not lawlessness in the name of the purity of Islam?"

The four walls of my room mocked my impotence. To whom could I say these things? Who would listen? I wept and cried out to the true God: "O, my God, show me the straight path!"

All this time I was working as an assistant to the Inspector in the Pakistan Postal Service. My duties were chiefly to look out for illegal materials, either in transit to other countries or destined for delivery in Pakistan. It was a shameful thing, but I found that many of my colleagues were doing a number of illegal things. For instance, when they found currency in envelopes (and it was against Pakistani law to send currency into the country by mail), instead of delivering it to the State

Bank of Pakistan as the rules demanded, they would keep it. Likewise, pornographic materials and other illegal literature was kept, instead of being destroyed. We would get requests from high officials asking us to send along the pornographic magazines to them and also to keep foreign currency for them.

I was also supposed to look out for anti-Islamic materials and to report them so that they could be destroyed. Being much more sympathetic to Christianity by this time, I used to read the Christian magazines and keep photostat copies of addresses so that I could write to these Christians myself, and in this way, I soon began to receive numerous magazines of many different theological viewpoints. I now think this may not have been very helpful, but at the time I was glad to learn from whatever source I could. But I must have imbibed quite a lot of useless ideas. Among other things, I read magazines from what I later learned to be false sects of Christianity, such as the Mormons, the Jehovah's Witnesses, the Jesus Only group and Christian Scientists. However, because I also read from sound Christian teachings, God kept me thinking about the truth, and it bore fruit later on.

And all the time I kept comparing. I compared the Islamic insistence on ritual cleanliness when one comes to God with the Christian concern that the heart of the worshipper be clean. John 4:24 spoke very clearly to me about this: "God is a Spirit: and they that worship him must worship him in spirit and in truth."

I think it was the issue of Christ's crucifixion which really taught me that God was able to show me directly what was the truth. I had read several books by this time, but real understanding was given to me from God Himself. It was by His Spirit, I now believe, that I was

able to see, from the Qur'an itself, that Jesus was crucified, that He died and that He ascended to heaven. This,
it seemed to me, was absolutely crucial, and I cried out
to God, "O God, if this were only true, then the day is not
far off when I will be an open Christian, acknowledging
that you are the true God and Father of the Lord Jesus
Christ."

I was dealing with three ideologies. First, the Christian creed that clearly asserted that Christ, the Messiah,
came into the world, was crucified, buried and raised on
the third day and ascended into heaven after forty days.
I understood this quite satisfactorily. Then there was
the orthodox Islamic teaching that Jesus Christ
ascended to heaven with His uncrucified body.

Then finally, the Ahmadi doctrines which I had
known since I was a child, that Christ was crucified, but
that He did not die on the cross, but rather swooned,
was revived and lived for many years thereafter in
Kashmir.

What I found perplexing was that both Islamic
groups "Proved" their point from the Qur'an. Ahmadi
teachings were at many points self-contradicting. They
could not agree on the details of Christ's death, and I
was inclined to dismiss their emphases because of this.
It would take too long to tell here, but there are at least
three different versions of the death of Christ, and at no
point do they agree.

And what of the Qur'an? It is said there in Sura 4
verse 157, "We slew the Messiah Jesus, son of Mary,
Allah's Messenger. They slew him not but it appeared so
unto them."

Islam holds that it is an awful disgrace for a prophet
to be killed, thus for Jesus to have been crucified would
have been intolerable. But in verse 155 the reference to

the Jews' unbelief and slaying of the prophets is very clear. So, I thought, how could a prophet not be a prophet simply because he lost his life in this calling? If anything, it seemed an honorable thing to me.

Then what is the truth of Christ's death, I wondered? Clearly, the answer is in the Bible; the same Bible that so many Muslims disbelieve, but at the same time use for their own commentaries and references. The answer is in Acts 2:22-36:

> Ye men of Israel, hear these words ... let all the house of Israel know assuredly, that God hath made that same Jesus, whom ye have crucified, both Lord and Christ.

Oh, I knew that Muslims disagreed about this, too. Some said that Judas Iscariot was slain in his place; others said Simon of Cyrene. But I knew that this could not be so. If it was Judas Iscariot, I thought, and if, as Muslims hold, God made his face to look like that of Jesus at that moment so that people were "taken in," would this not be intolerable deception? Why did Judas not cry out or make a noise? Is God a fraud that He should engage in such a charade? My whole being refused to accept that idea.

But what of Simon of Cyrene? Many Muslims believe that because he was carrying the cross of Jesus the people were confused and thought that it was Jesus Himself, and so crucified Simon instead! But again my mind refused to believe it. How could Jesus, the true Prophet of God, have allowed such a terrible deception? It was unthinkable. Further, if the story of Jesus' crucifixion is just a story, then what is one to make of the character of the disciples? How could they lie like that? How could they preach about love and obedience to God if they knew that they were agreeing to a lie of such immense proportions? It was unthinkable. How could such hypocrites have any fruit on this earth or in heaven?

No, I concluded, the Qur'an and the Hadith had agreed that Jesus was truly crucified, died and was taken to God. And I found to my total satisfaction that as far as the Bible was concerned Jesus had, in His own person, fulfilled the Old Testament prophecies. I closed my books, my research was at an end, and it was time for me to consider what the next step should be.

_____ 12 _____

Into the Light of the Son

The very next Sunday, I was in the church with the other Christians singing the hymn *"How great Thou Art"* with all my heart! The words rang in my soul, and I was forced to face the meaning of them if I was to be honest.

"Masood," I said to myself as the hymn finished and we all sat down, "you can't keep two swords in one scabbard; you can't serve two different masters like this. You must decide. Who will you follow? Will it be Muhammad or Jesus? Whoever it is, you must make the choice soon—as soon as possible."

I knew this was true, but my situation was very difficult. It was clear that should I decide to follow Jesus the Christ, I would be repudiated by my family and friends forever, and if I am honest, I must admit that I still had a small hope that I might continue in Islam, but as a true believer in Jesus Christ.

In the final analysis it seemed to be a theological problem. Islam called me to acknowledge the One True God and Muhammad, His Prophet, and to perform good deeds in order to be saved. But if I were to follow Christ, then he must do it all for me; there was no way that I could save myself.

Islam wanted to tell me how I could keep God happy with me, but Christianity emphasized what Christ had done, once and for all, to reconcile mankind with God. I knew my sinful nature made it impossible for me to please God myself.

The Qur'an portrayed itself to me as guidance for those who are pious, those who are not bad or evil, but the Bible made it abundantly plain that it was the word of life to sinners of whom even the great Apostle Paul could say, "I am the chief."

Above all, the Person of Christ was the focal point. Without Him, the whole edifice of Christianity would collapse like a mud-brick building in an earthquake. But Muhammad is portrayed in the Qur'an simply as "a messenger [the like of whom] have passed before him" (Sura 3 verse 144). There was such a difference in their personalities.

As the preacher continued to speak, I saw a vision of myself having left everything to search for the truth. And now, when it seemed that I had found it, I was caught between two mighty, opposing forces. I hesitated to leap forward, but when I looked back, I saw only the distress and legalism of Islam. I heard Christ out in front of me: "Follow me and I will give you rest."

But at the same time, I was afraid of what the Qureshi family would think of me. Would they see me as an ungrateful fellow who had abused their hospitality and goodness? I had never known such caring love as I had in that home. They had met my need when I was helpless, lost and dying. Even now they seemed, in their goodness, to be as "angels" to me—messengers from God bringing physical help as the ravens brought bread to Elijah when he was hiding from Ahab. What would be the result if now I were to confess to them that I was going to be a Christian? My heart wavered in uncertainty.

I was reading both the Bible and the Qur'an, expecting to get light from both. I was going to church, but also quite regularly to the mosque. I listened to Christian pastors and also to the *mawlawis*. And all the time I knew that I had to decide.

I had a radio in my room. It belonged to the Qureshis, but they had kindly allowed me to use it since I had come to live with them. I used to listen regularly to the Christian broadcasts put out by the Far East Broadcasting Association (FEBA) ever since Mr. Massey had told me about these programs.

The Qureshis used to listen to them occasionally, but they were not very interested, and the evening programs were often hard to get anyway, as Moscow Radio broadcasts on almost the same frequency.

One morning, I was listening to the radio as I got ready to go to work. A certain preacher was discussing the kingdom of heaven; I was listening with only one ear, but at the end of his message he mentioned a few verses from the Bible that shocked me:

> Therefore take no thought, saying, 'What shall we eat or What shall we drink?' or, 'Wherewithal shall we be clothed' … for your heavenly Father knoweth that ye have need of all these things. But seek ye first the kingdom of God, and his righteousness; and all these things shall be added unto you (Matthew 6:31-33).

These words spoke right to my heart. "How well the Father knows the hearts of His children," I thought. Only He could have known that I had been very fearful about being put out of the Qureshis' home to wander to and fro again without shelter or food. Only He could know how this thought affected me. Now I knew that if it was required of me I would even be able to accept this.

That day I took three days' leave from work, and all those long hours I kept hearing the words from Matthew's gospel ringing in my ears. I don't believe I prayed all that day. I was waiting for God to somehow reveal Himself to me (as though He had not already done so!). I see now that this was a thought that did not come from God. And other words from the Bible came unbidden, "Have I been so long time with you, and yet hast thou not known me?" (John 14:9).

I opened the Bible and found these words in John's gospel and read the whole paragraph carefully (John 14:5-9). The words seemed to apply absolutely to me, and I felt myself being torn apart, unable to let go and trust Him completely.

In front of me there was a mirror, but I could not bear to look myself in the face. Elsewhere in the house, I heard the bustle of the Qureshi family as they came and went, but I was alone with my own thoughts and fears. Mentally, I reviewed my research again, and I could see no way out for me. It was all so clear.

The same God who said to me in my childhood, "Study in this school for now, and when you finish it, I will give you admission to my school," was waiting to do it—and I was afraid. The same God who lovingly engineered my circumstances so that I might discover the truth was waiting for me—and I was holding back. "Might I not be in danger of testing Him too far?" I thought in sudden panic. And overwhelmed, I burst out weeping.

Close to exhaustion, I think I must have slept, for suddenly a light flashed in the room, and it seemed to my feverish mind that the wall had disappeared. There was an old, old scene that I recognized immediately, and seeing it I recalled the incident in chapter 20 of the gospel of John. I saw Thomas sitting with the other Apostles. He looked upset and doubtful. Then suddenly I saw Jesus in the midst of them all and He said, "Peace be unto you." I noticed that Thomas's mouth was hanging open with surprise.

Then Jesus was saying to Thomas, "Reach hither thy finger, and behold my hands; and reach hither thy hand, and thrust it into my side: and be not faithless, but believing." It was then that Thomas fell at the feet of Jesus and said, "My Lord and my God." At that, Jesus took him by the hand and raised him to his feet and said, "Thomas because thou hast seen me, thou hast believed: blessed are they that have not seen, and yet have believed."

The scene faded and vanished. I found myself standing still in my room, and I began to think over what I had seen and heard in my dream. I understood all too well what the message to me was. I was like Thomas, skeptical and unbelieving, and now Jesus had shown that He loved me still and invited me to follow Him.

All at once, I felt a great sorrow. "He was at the door of my heart all that time," I whispered aloud, "and I did not open to Him." I felt that Satan had won an easy victory because I had not been on my guard against him. How could I have listened to him, when the Lord of the whole universe had been knocking at the door of my heart?

Slowly the light dawned, and I slipped to my knees and cried out, "O Lord, I do believe. Forgive my stubbornness and skepticism and receive me."

And I heard a gentle voice within me say, "As many as I love, I rebuke and chasten: be zealous therefore, and repent" (Revelation 3:19).

I rose from my knees a changed person. It seemed to me that my whole being was singing "How great Thou art," and the peace of mind, the rest, the security that I experienced that night, April 26th, 1973, I had never known before. More than two years of research and study found their fulfillment in the revelation to my soul that Jesus Christ was my Lord and my God, to the glory of God the Father.

The very next day, I went to see Mr. Massey. He was not at home, so I sat in a nearby restaurant drinking tea until he came. My heart was light. When I rang the bell again he came to the door, very surprised to see me. "Why, Masood, you seem different today," he observed, and I was happy to assure him that I was! He drew me by the arm into his house and led me to the drawing room. I had not sat there before, and I remember thinking what a pleasant room it was, with its freshly color-washed walls and homely atmosphere.

Mr. Massey was speaking to me, "How are your Bible studies coming along, Masood?" he asked kindly.

I looked him straight in the eye, and in the words of the Ethiopian eunuch, I asked him simply, "What doth hinder me to be baptized?" (Acts 8:36).

He understood my meaning, but returned my look unsmiling. "You know what this may mean, Masood?" "I understand," I said, "and God will help me." But Mr. Massey was still worried. "What about death, Masood?" he asked urgently. "Whosoever killeth you will think that he doeth God a service" (John 16:2).

But the peace of God was very real at that moment.

"Even then I will remember Christ who said, 'Father, forgive them; for they know not what they do'" (Luke 23:34).

Hearing these words, he came forward and embraced me, holding me tightly to himself. With his arms around me, he prayed for me, and when he had finished he stood back, holding me at arms' length.

"This is a happy day for me, Masood," he said.

We talked about my being baptized. He said that he would go on my behalf and talk with the pastor about it, but I insisted on going with him there and then. We walked together to the church and spoke with Mr. Vincent. He expressed his delight at the outcome of my research, and we eventually decided that the baptism would be carried out the next Sunday. He was of the opinion that I should be baptized in front of only a few Christians, but I insisted on it taking place during the regular worship, and so it happened.

It was Sunday evening, April 29, 1973. The church was full of worshippers when the announcement was made that there was to be a baptism that evening. Everyone looked round when I stood up and made my way forward to the pulpit. Behind me stood Mr. Massey. I was introduced from the pulpit briefly by Mr. Vincent though not much was said about my background. Of course it was clear that I was a Muslim seeking baptism, and this, in itself, was unusual enough. In fact, this was the last baptism Mr. Vincent performed in Karachi, for soon afterwards he was transferred to a Pakistani church in Southall, London, and later died there.

As the baptism service progressed, my mind was wandering and thinking about the disciples of Jesus who were commanded:

Go ye therefore, and teach all nations, baptizing them in the name of the Father, and of the Son, and of the Holy Ghost: Teaching them to observe all things whatsoever I have commanded you (Matthew 28:19-20).

As I was baptized I could hear the distant voice of Mr. Vincent. "I baptize you in the name of the Father and the Son and the Holy Spirit." A few years ago those words were of no significance to me, but today I could feel it; I could comprehend what the Scripture said:

> So many of us as were baptized into Jesus Christ were baptized into his death. Therefore we are buried with him by baptism into death: that like as Christ was raised up from the dead by the glory of the Father, even so we also should walk in newness of life (Romans 6:3-4).

After the service, everyone gathered around to greet me. Mr. Massey introduced me to various friends, and in the rush we were separated. After most of the people had drifted off, I waited outside the church for him, and while I was there I noticed three young men chatting together. Another boy joined them, and I could not help overhearing the conversation.

"I've been waiting for you and here you are still," he began, looking around. "What's the matter? Has the worship ended late?"

"Yes, my friend," said one of the young men. "Today a *Musla* [a bad name for a Muslim] has become a Christian."

The young fellow looked interested.

"Where is he now?" he demanded. "Let's see him."

"Oh, we weren't at the service," they said. "We've just come from Koshal's house and haven't seen him. But we'll meet him one day I suppose."

How quickly discouragement comes! Hearing myself called by that horrible name, my heart sank, and I was ready to slink away when Mr. Massey came around the corner. He hurried when he saw me.

"Ah, there you are, Masood," he said with a smile. "Come over here and meet these young men."

It was clear that they knew Mr. Massey well, and they gaped, somewhat confused, when I was introduced. They realized that I must have overheard them, and they shuffled their feet uneasily.

That evening, when I arrived home, I was a little afraid that perhaps I would be questioned by the Qureshis, but everything was as usual.

My room, as always, was clean and neat, and the books which I had left lying untidily on my bed had been put back in their places. It was all very homely, and yet I wondered whether I could possibly continue to be at home in this place where I had been so happy. As I came out of the bathroom after changing my clothes I noticed, hanging on the back of a chair, the *ja Namaz*, the prayer rug on which a Muslim can say his prayers when he can't get to a mosque. I thought of the many times I had prayed, kneeling on this rug, and I thought, too, of the kindness of Mrs. Qureshi who had given it to me a year ago—a special gift from the holy city of Medina. How many times I had prayed kneeling there, "God, show me the straight path."

With a decisive gesture, I took the rug from the chair and put it into the cupboard. Praise God, I was now on the straight path, and I could come to God at anytime, anywhere, under any circumstance. I felt free!

What about the Qur'an, I wondered? My eyes focused on the much-studied book on my desk. Should it also go into the cupboard to be forgotten? Would I have no need for it? In my heart I knew that I could not do this. This book was a witness to my Muslim friends. I knew that when I was asked about my faith, I would be able to tell how I had discovered Jesus Christ in the pages of that book. It was the Qur'an that had kept me searching for the truth, and I determined that I would give it a place in my testimony.

That night before I slept, I opened the Bible and read from Matthew 10:1 & 23:

> Behold, I send you forth as sheep ... for verily I say unto you, Ye shall not have gone over the cities of Israel, till the Son of Man be come.

I thanked Him for this message, turned over and slept like a child.

13

Moving On

It was not long before the Qureshi family noticed that I was not attending the mosque for prayers and that I did not pray at home in the Islamic fashion either. They began to suspect that I had lost my faith, and one day Mr. and Mrs. Qureshi asked me straight out. I could not deny it and admitted that I had become a Christian. They were very upset, and over the next few weeks their behavior towards me changed dramatically.

By this time it was all over my office that I had trusted in Christ. Some of my colleagues thought that I had been taken in by a foreign missionary who had promised to give me a good job or take me abroad if I renounced Islam. Yet some would ask quite genuine questions, and it was a wonderful opportunity for me to share something of what Christ meant to me.

The arguments, however, continued at home as well as at the office, and one day, finally accepting that I was irrevocably committed to Christ, the Qureshis told me that it was time I moved out and arranged for my own living.

I had to spend that last night in their servants' quarters, and it felt to me as if another chapter of my life was ending. That night when I knelt for prayer I said to my heavenly Father, "Father, if it is your will that I be on the road again, I have no objections."

I felt that He accepted this prayer, and as I lay down to sleep on the hard floor, for the first time in almost four years with the Qureshis, memories of the old days came flooding back. Finally I fell asleep, and when I woke it was full daylight. Indecision pulled at me as I thought to myself, "Masood, there's still time. Go and beg their pardon and be reconciled with this family that loves you. Think what you're giving up. Think of your job, your future ..." But then I remembered the Lord Jesus, how He went into the wilderness and lived for forty days and nights. I remembered His words to Satan, "Thou shalt worship the Lord thy God, and him only shalt thou serve."

Immediately I jumped up, hurriedly took my bag and slipped quietly out of the room. At the gate I paused and looked at the house that had been home to me for such a long time, and then I was in the street. I set off down the road.

I did not look back.

Over the years since I became a Christian, my relatives, friends and colleagues have often accused me of being a traitor to the Muslim community and my country, of being disobedient to my parents, and of blasphemy by believing in three gods. This complete lack of understanding of the Christian faith, and of the Bible which so many Muslims actively fear to read, pains my heart. It is clearly written that Christians must submit themselves to earthly authorities (I Peter 2:13-14), honor their parents (Exodus 20:12), and believe and trust in the one true God (Matthew 22:37).

Even fellow Christians have treated me with suspicion; some because I was not a member of their particular denomination, some because they believed that I had become a Christian solely for material gain, and others because they regarded me as a government agent sent to spy on the church!

Wherever I went, I always testified to my love of the Lord Jesus, and this often cost me my job. Time and again I would be turned out from work or lodgings with the cry of—"Get out, you filthy sweeper, and don't come back!" Yet above all this I felt a great peace. I remembered and shared in the rejection Christ suffered, and often the Spirit of God would bring the word to my mind to comfort and strengthen me: "Except a corn of wheat fall into the ground and die, it abideth alone; but if it die, it bringeth forth much fruit" (John 12:24).

Troubles, persecution, suffering; yes, certainly I have experienced these. Several years after my conversion, my father wanted to follow the order of capital punishment for apostates in Islam, but the Lord saved me. At university campus a few years later, not liking my testimony and conversations of how I chose to follow Jesus, some fanatic students kidnapped me, drugged me and buried me alive, but the Lord rescued me. People ask me, "Are you really satisfied with this wandering life? Are you happy to live as a fugitive for the rest of your days? Is that the reason you did your research?"

No, the reason for my research was ever to find the truth, that truth which would set me free from the empty way of life handed down by my forefathers. And God Himself opened my heart and mind to the straight path, the way He chose before the creation of the world through which mankind could be reconciled with Him—Jesus Christ, who shared in our humanity so that by His death He might destroy Satan and free those who all their lives have been held in slavery.

Since becoming a Christian I have become acutely aware of my unworthiness, but at the same time I know that in God's eyes my value is great. That is why He tells me through His word:

> I say unto you, Take no thought for your life, what ye shall eat, or what ye shall drink; nor yet for your body, what ye shall put on. Is not the life more than meat, and the body than raiment? Behold the fowls of the air: for they sow not, neither do they reap, nor gather into barns; yet your heavenly Father feedeth them. Are ye not much better than they? (Matthew 6:25-26).

I know that this life I have is not my own. I have given it willingly to Jesus, and He knows what is best for me. Although I have lost my worldly family, and although there have been threats against me, my Lord comforts me:

> And fear not them which kill the body, but are not able to kill the soul: but rather fear him which is able to destroy both soul and body in hell. Are not two sparrows sold for a farthing? and one of them shall not fall on the ground without your Father. ... Fear ye not therefore, ye are of more value than many sparrows (Matthew 10:28-29, 31).

In all of life's troubles, perplexities and temptations, and in loneliness, weariness and disappointments, it is He who comes to rescue us, and I praise Him for this. Like the Apostle Paul, I am able to say: "Even though I am beaten, yet I am not killed; though at times I am sorrowful, yet I am always rejoicing; though poor, I have been given the opportunity to make many rich by sharing the gospel; though I have nothing, yet as a child of God I possess everything; should I die, yet will I live on. I can consider everything a loss compared to the surpassing greatness of *knowing* Christ Jesus my Lord.

He does not want anyone to perish, but wants all to be saved and to come to a knowledge of the truth" (see I Timothy 2:3-4).

"To day if ye will hear his voice, harden not your hearts" (Hebrews 4:7; Psalm 95:7-8).

Other Books by the Author

The Bible and the Qur'an: A Question of Integrity

Why follow Jesus?

More than Conquerors

For information about having Dr. Steven Masood
speak at your church, fellowship, conference or an
event, contact: ITL-USA, P. O. Box 1555, Summer-
field, FL 34492

e-mail: sm@itl-usa.org